I0415744

Operational-Level Logistics

U.S. Marine Corps

PCN 143 000099 00

DISTRIBUTION STATEMENT A: Approved for public; distribution is unlimited

To Our Readers

Changes: Readers of this publication are encouraged to submit suggestions and changes that will improve it. Recommendations may be sent directly to Commanding General, Marine Corps Combat Development Command, Doctrine Division (C 42), 3300 Russell Road, Suite 318A, Quantico, VA 22134-5021 or by fax to 703-784-2917 (DSN 278-2917) or by E-mail to **morgann@mccdc.usmc.mil**. Recommendations should include the following information:

ı Location of change
  Publication number and title
  Current page number
  Paragraph number (if applicable)
  Line number
  Figure or table number (if applicable)
ı Nature of change
  Add, delete
  Proposed new text, preferably double-spaced and typewritten
ı Justification and/or source of change

Additional copies: A printed copy of this publication may be obtained from Marine Corps Logistics Base, Albany, GA 31704-5001, by following the instructions in MCBul 5600, *Marine Corps Doctrinal Publications Status.* An electronic copy may be obtained from the Doctrine Division, MCCDC, world wide web home page which is found at the following universal reference locator: **http://www.doctrine.usmc.mil**.

**Unless otherwise stated, whenever the masculine gender is used,
both men and women are included.**

DEPARTMENT OF THE NAVY
Headquarters United States Marine Corps
Washington, D.C. 20308-1775

30 January 2002

FOREWORD

Marine Corps Warfighting Publication (MCWP) 4-12, *Operational-Level Logistics,* addresses fundamental principles for the planning and execution of logistics for the Marine Corps component within a theater of operations; the relationships between the Marine Corps forces (MARFOR) logistics staff, the Marine Logistics Command (MLC), Marine expeditionary force (MEF) logistics staff, and the force service support group (FSSG); and coordination with external theater logistic agencies. MCWP 4-12 delineates the division of labor between MLC and FSSG by providing logistics employment guidance. In addition, this publication identifies strategic logistic organizations and agencies that provide support to MARFOR in theater. MCWP 4-12 expands on MCWP 4-1, *Logistics Operations*, by providing detailed guidance to Marine Corps logisticians who conduct operational logistics.

This publication is a detailed guide for field grade action officers serving on MARFOR, MEF, and FSSG staffs, who are responsible for planning and conducting logistics at the operational level. The secondary audience is comprised of commanders and staff officers who require logistic support or who will benefit from a greater understanding of theater-level logistics.

Reviewed and approved this date.

BY DIRECTION OF THE COMMANDANT OF THE MARINE CORPS

EDWARD HANLON, JR.
Lieutenant General, U.S. Marine Corps
Commanding General
Marine Corps Combat Development Command

DISTRIBUTION: 143 000099 00

OPERATIONAL-LEVEL LOGISTICS
TABLE OF CONTENTS

Chapter 5 Operations

Chapter 6 Strategic Support

Chapter 7 Logistic Vision

Appendices

CHAPTER 1. FUNDAMENTALS

Military operations require specific logistic support, and that support is based on the strategic, operational, and tactical levels of war. Operational-level logistics links strategic resources with tactical units and enables force closure, sustainment, reconstitution, and redeployment of forces. Functions of operational logistics are normally carried out in the communications zone (COMMZ), which is the rear part of a theater of operations contiguous to the combat zone. Operational logistics supports expeditionary operations.

The levels of logistics assist Marines in planning for logistics at the corresponding levels of warfare. Operational-level logistics addresses sustainment within a military theater of operations. Operational-level logistics connects strategic-level logistic resources with the tactical level of logistics thus creating the conditions for effective Marine air-ground task force (MAGTF) combat service support (CSS) for the duration of a campaign. Understanding operational-level logistics is critical to integrated planning and the successful conduct of expeditionary operations.

Operational Logistic Environment

Marine Corps forces (MARFOR) conducting expeditionary operations as part of a joint force will be under the command of a joint force commander (JFC). The MARFOR plans, coordinates, and supervises the execution of operational (theater) logistics for the assigned MAGTF. Each Service provides administrative and logistic support to its forces assigned or attached to a joint force. The JFC may have the authority to direct a single Service to provide common item logistics to components of the joint force. Consequently, the MARFOR coordinates operational logistic support for the MAGTF per Marine Corps Service responsibility and for other Service components as directed by the JFC.

Joint doctrine encourages inter-Service support, which is defined as action taken by one Service or element thereof, to provide logistics and/or administrative support to another Service. The relationship between the Navy and Marine Corps is a recurring association that affects the Marine Corps at all levels of war.

Joint forces with a MARFOR assigned or attached include a Marine Corps component. The Marine Corps component commander provides administrative and logistic support for the MARFOR with the exceptions of logistics provided through service support agreements or as directed by the JFC.

The joint force and its Service components may conduct expeditionary operations as part of a multinational force (MNF). Formal treaties have resulted in military alliances that have produced multinational military organizations, procedures, and responsibilities that guide participating forces. North Atlantic Treaty Organization (NATO) and the United Nations Forces in Korea are two long-term alliances in which U.S. Forces participate. Short-term threats produce coalitions where the military forces of different nations temporarily cooperate to accomplish an agreed mission. Logistics remains a national responsibility; however, nations may cooperate and make support arrangements to increase efficiency and economy.

MARFOR logistic planners coordinate with other Services, Department of Defense (DOD) logistic agencies, and governmental and nongovernmental organizations (NGOs) to meet requirements. Joint force operations may interact with interagency organizations, especially during military operations other than war (MOOTW). Interagency coordination occurs between elements of the DOD and engaged U.S. Government agencies, NGOs, and regional and international organizations to accomplish an objective. The MARFOR can expect to receive operational logistic assistance from the United States Transportation Command (USTRANSCOM),

Defense Logistics Agency (DLA), and other strategic logistic agencies.

Logistic Continuum

Joint doctrine divides a continuum of war into strategic, operational, and tactical levels. Each level of war has a corresponding level of logistics with a distinct set of functions. Figure 1-1 lists the logistic functions for the levels of operations within the logistic operating system.

Strategic

Strategic logistics supports organizing, training, and equipping the forces that are needed to further the national interest. It links the national economic base (people, resources, and industry) to military operations. The combination of strategic resources (national industrial base) and distribution processes (deployment and transportation capabilities) represents total national capabilities. These capabilities include the DOD, the Services, other Government agencies as necessary or appropriate, and the support of the private sector.

Headquarters, Marine Corps (HQMC), and the Marine Corps supporting establishment (SE) plan and conduct strategic logistics, with the exception of aviation-peculiar support, which is planned and conducted by the Chief of Naval Operations (CNO), the Navy SE, and the Naval Reserve.

Operational

Operational logistics links tactical requirements to strategic capabilities to accomplish operational goals and objectives. Operational logistics normally supports campaigns and major theater operations by providing theater-wide logistic support. Operational logisticians coordinate the apportionment, allocation, and distribution of resources within theater. They coordinate closely with tactical operators to identify theater shortfalls and communicate these shortfalls to the appropriate theater or strategic source and/or ration supplies to support operational priorities. Operational logisticians coordinate the flow of strategic capabilities into a theater based on the commander's priorities. The concerns of the logistician and the operator are interrelated. The MARFOR is responsible for planning, coordinating, and supervising operational logistics. The

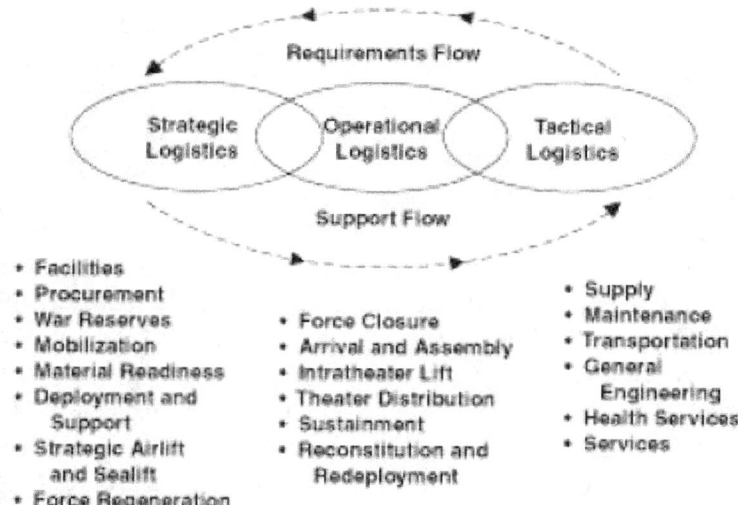

Figure 1-1. Logistic Functions.

MARFOR may designate a combat service support element (CSSE) to be a Marine Logistics Command (MLC) to coordinate the execution of operational logistics.

Tactical

Tactical logistics includes organic unit capabilities and the CSS activities necessary to support military operations. It supports the commander's concept of operations while maximizing the commander's flexibility and freedom of action. Tactical logistics involves the coordination of functions required to sustain and move units, personnel, equipment, and supplies. The response time of tactical logistics is rapid and requires anticipatory planning to provide responsive support. Generally, the MAGTF conducts tactical-level logistic operations. Figure 1-2 shows the flow of logistics through the logistic system from the strategic to tactical level.

Functions

Force closure, arrival and assembly, intratheater lift, theater distribution, sustainment, reconstitution, and redeployment are the primary functions of operational-level logistics.

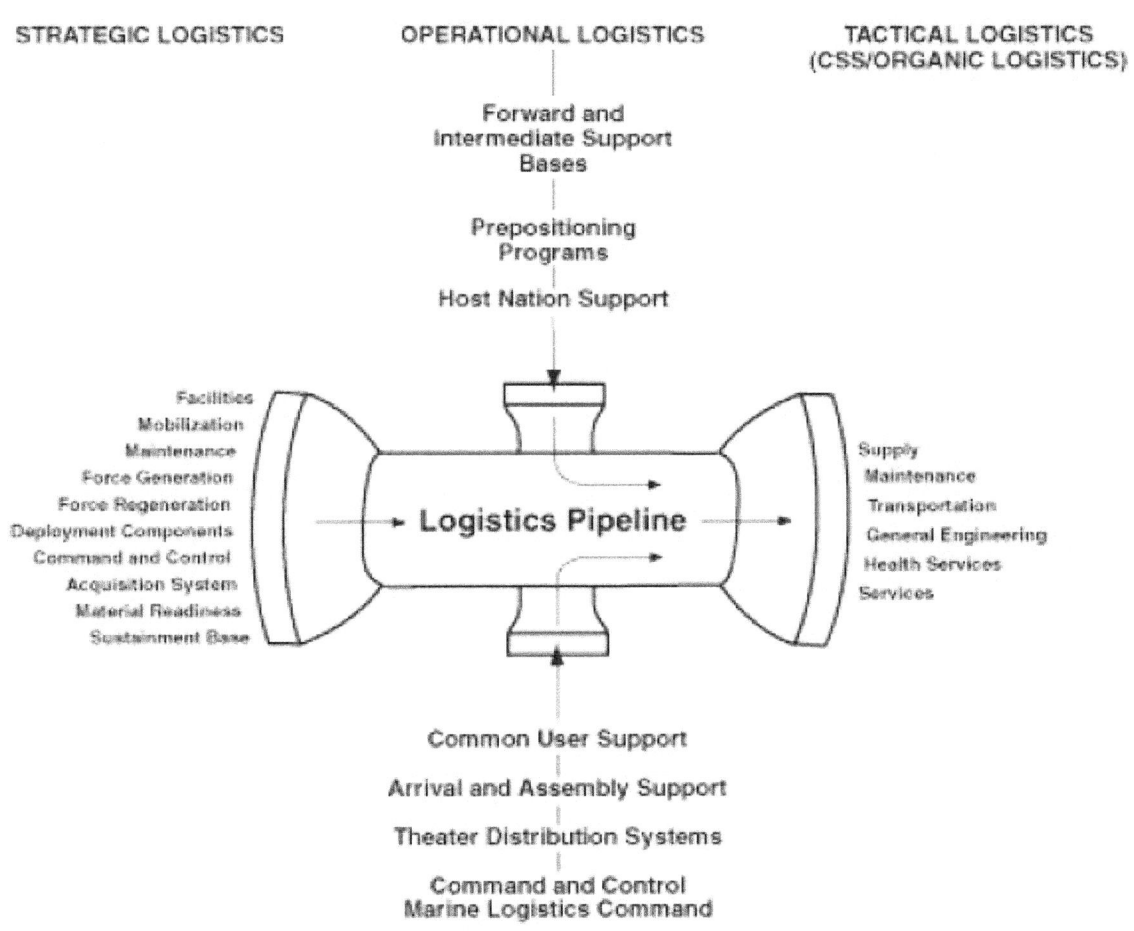

Figure 1-2. Logistic System.

Force Closure

Force closure is when a supported commander determines that sufficient personnel and equipment are in the area of operations (AO) to carry out assigned tasks. The Marine Corps/Navy team has developed the lead capability for force closure in hostile and uncertain environments.

Arrival and Assembly

Arrival and assembly is the most critical phase of force closure. It begins on the arrival of the first ship or the first aircraft of the main body at a designated arrival and assembly area (AAA). Arrival and assembly ends when adequate equipment and supplies are off-loaded and issued to awaiting units, command and control (C2) is established, and the MAGTF commander reports that essential elements of the MAGTF have attained combat readiness.

Reception, staging, onward movement, and integration (RSOI) is intended to transition arriving personnel and materiel into forces capable of meeting operational requirements and aims to reduce confusion associated with personnel and equipment arriving in-theater in disjointed pieces. RSOI should reduce bottlenecks at theater points of entry that have existed in large-scale joint operations. Since MAGTFs phase into theater as organized, combat-ready units, they ordinarily require only limited arrival and assembly operations vice full RSOI. The MARFOR must coordinate MAGTF force closure operations with the JFC within a joint RSOI framework. Table 1-1 portrays a likely progression of force closure in a theater of operations.

Intratheater Lift

Intratheater lift is the sum of all transportation modes in a theater of war that are available for the MARFOR to move, sustain, and redeploy forces. Intratheater lift consists of the trucks, buses, trains,

aircraft, pipelines, ships, lighterage, vessels, and ferries available to support MARFOR. The MARFOR coordinates lift support for the MAGTF.

Theater Distribution

The theater distribution network consists of the physical network and resources that facilitate distribution. Theater distribution is the flow of personnel, equipment, and materiel within a theater of operation that enables the MAGTF to accomplish its tactical missions. Component responsibility for ground theater distribution and coastal/inland waterways normally rests with the Army component, while the Air Force component usually plans and coordinates distribution by air. The MARFOR assists coordination between theater distribution assets and procedures and MAGTF requirements and capabilities.

The physical network of the distribution system consists of the quantity, capacity, and capability of fixed structures and established facilities available to support distribution operations. It includes roads, airfields, railroads, hardened structures (e.g., warehouses, storage facilities), seaports, inland waterways, and pipelines.

The resource network of the distribution system consists of the personnel (uniformed and civilian—host nation, government, military, and contractor), organizations, materiel, and equipment operating within the physical network of the distribution system.

Table 1-1. Progression of Force Closure Operations.

Initial Phase of Deployment	Later Phase of Deployment	Mature Phase of Deployment
Marine Corps/Navy	Service components	Joint
Forced entry/maritime pre-positioning force (MPF)	RSOI/joint logistics over-the-shore (JLOTS)	Joint RSOI

Sustainment

Sustainment is the provision of personnel, logistics, and other support required to maintain and prolong operations or combat to the successful accomplishment of or revision to the mission or the national objective. Sustainment is made up of assets deployed as accompanying supplies and follow-on supplies as required by the JFC's concept of operations. The sustainment moves via theater distribution and intratheater lift.

Reconstitution

Reconstitution is the regeneration, reorganization, replenishment, and reorientation of a MAGTF for a new mission without having to return to home base. Reconstitution is largely a function of command and operations, but CSS units conduct the actual resupply, maintenance, retrograde, and medical functions. The MLC will execute these functions, when established, per MARFOR guidance. Personnel replacement is also a key component of reconstitution. In addition to normal support actions, reconstitution may include—

● Removing a unit from combat.
● Assessing the unit with external assets.
● Reestablishing the chain of command.
● Training the unit for future operations.
● Reestablishing unit cohesion.

There are two types of reconstitution: reorganization and regeneration. Reorganization is usually accomplished in an expeditious manner at the tactical unit level by rapid assessment of combat essential assets on hand and redistribution as necessary for maximum combat effectiveness. It includes assistance from the direct support (DS) CSS unit. Regeneration is more deliberate, requiring more time and assistance from the MARFOR and the strategic sustainment base.

Redeployment

Redeployment is the transfer of a unit, individual, or supplies deployed in one area to another area, or another location within the area for the purpose of further employment.

Functional Area Responsibilities

The MARFOR identifies and sources the best resources for each of the six logistic functional areas (i.e., supply, maintenance, transportation, general engineering, health service support [HSS], and services). The MARFOR coordinates support within each logistic function per Marine Corps Service responsibilities; joint force policy/operations order; mission, enemy, terrain and weather, troops and support available-time available (METT-T); and the MAGTF commander's concept of operations and intent.

Supply

The MARFOR supply concept divides sustainment into periods supported by accompanying supplies and follow-on sustainment. A MAGTF deploys with a block of accompanying supplies to sustain operations in a theater until follow-on sustainment arrives. The duration of support provided by accompanying supplies varies based on MAGTF size and mission assigned. Actual movement of sustainment starts when the operation begins and continues until the termination of the operation. The MARFOR has the following supply responsibilities:

● Identifying, prioritizing, sourcing, and coordinating the delivery of unsourced requirements in the MAGTF's accompanying supplies.
● Identifying, prioritizing, sourcing, and coordinating the flow of resupply for the MAGTF.
● Registering the war reserve withdraw plan to meet the MAGTF commander's unsourced requirements.
● Identifying, sourcing, and coordinating the flow of supplies needed to reconstitute and redeploy the MAGTF.
● Coordinating common-user logistic supply support.

- Contracting goods and services from the local economy.
- Coordinating MAGTF contingency contracting support plans with higher headquarters (HHQ).
- Ensuring that MAGTF supply buildup rates and stockage levels comply with joint force guidance.
- Ensuring the JFC allocates critical resources to the MAGTF.
- Communicating with appropriate headquarters on supply matters and related requirements.
- Coordinating the provision of common-item support with the MAGTF when designated by the JFC.

Maintenance

Maintenance is a Service responsibility. The MARFOR identifies and prioritizes maintenance requirements that exceed the MAGTF's authorized level of maintenance and/or capacity to repair, modify or calibrate. The JFC may establish joint, multinational or cross-Service maintenance facilities for common-item and inter-Service salvage operations. The MARFOR ensures that theater common-item maintenance support is linked to MAGTF maintenance operations. The MARFOR plans and coordinates surge maintenance operations with the Marine Corps SE for regeneration operations before MAGTF redeployment.

Transportation

The MARFOR coordinates MAGTF force closure and redeployment operations within the Defense Transportation System (DTS). The theater transportation function spans all modes of transportation (i.e., air, motor vehicle, rail, water, and pipeline) within the distribution system. The MAGTF submits movement support requirements through the force movement control centers (FMCCs) to the appropriate joint or Service movement control center (MCC). In some cases,

the theater transportation and MCC may coordinate theater transportation down to the level of tactical convoys. The MARFOR may serve as part of a Joint Transportation Board (JTB) or joint movement center (JMC).

The MARFOR would coordinate designated transportation and transportation support operations for the MAGTF. The MARFOR has the following transportation responsibilities:

- Coordinating MAGTF throughput operations with the host nation, joint, and/or inter-Service agency.
- Linking the MAGTF's movement control system with the joint and/or multinational movement control system.
- Coordinating MAGTF requirements for common-user land and inland waterway transportation with the Army Service component commander.
- Coordinating with the Air Force Service component commander for theater common user airlift.
- Coordinating with the Navy Service component commander through Military Sealift Command (MSC) for common-user sealift.
- Ensuring the theater medical evacuation system is responsive to MAGTF requirements.
- Assigning liaison officers (LNOs) to essential transportation nodes operated by another component or host nation.
- Planning and coordinating MAGTF surge requirements such as the evacuation of mass casualties and enemy prisoners of war (EPWs) from the combat zone and the relocation of the MAGTF within the theater of war.
- Ensuring the theater transportation system can meet MAGTF requirements for moving bulk liquids, outsized cargo and equipment, and intermodal containerization.
- Ensuring responsive transportation is available to move critical items such as blood, precision munitions, and repair parts from the COMMZ to the MAGTF.

General Engineering

Engineering requirements normally increase during MAGTF force closure. The addition of a naval mobile construction battalion (NMCB) and an expeditionary airfield capability to each MPF through the MPF enhancement program has increased the capability of operational-level engineers. In addition to force closure, the MARFOR has the following general engineering responsibilities:

- Identifying and prioritizing vertical and horizontal engineering projects.
- Managing facilities.
- Assessing environmental impact of MAGTF operations.
- Coordinating utilities, bulk liquids support, and explosive ordnance disposal.

Health Service Support

The MARFOR is responsible for coordinating and integrating HSS in the theater of war. This function requires the integration of the MAGTF's HSS with theater HSS capabilities. MARFOR has the following HSS responsibilities:

- Coordinating with the joint force surgeon (JFS).
- Establishing links between the MAGTF and theater HSS agencies.
- Coordinating medical regulating for patients above level II facilities with the senior theater medical regulating agency.
- Ensuring adequate supplies of blood and blood products.

- Identifying, prioritizing, sourcing, and coordinating shortfalls in the MAGTF's block of accompanying medical/dental supplies.
- Ensuring the flow of medical supplies to the MAGTF.
- Repairing or replacing broken or damaged medical equipment that exceeds the maintenance capabilities of the MAGTF.
- Ensuring the smooth exchange of medical intelligence between the MAGTF and the joint force/other components.
- Monitoring the medical personnel and augmentation system, hospital ship deployment, and military blood program, as appropriate.

Services

Disbursing, postal, legal, security support, exchange, and limited mortuary affairs are services organic to the Marine expeditionary force (MEF). Marine Corps civil affairs and mortuary affairs capabilities reside in the Reserve Establishment and requires significant Army augmentation. The MARFOR is concerned with establishing the links between MAGTF services providers and the agencies responsible for theater-level support. MAGTF postal, graves registration, exchange, and EPW holding capabilities are linked to Army agencies, which normally provide theater-level support to the joint force. The MARFOR may absorb the legal services, civil affairs, and disbursing capabilities of the MAGTF to focus on facilitating host-nation and coalition relations, contingency contracting, and the development of inter-Service and multinational support agreements, while providing general support (GS) to the MAGTF.

CHAPTER 2. THEATER ORGANIZATIONS

The theater logistic environment contains many organizations that have potential roles and responsibilities during expeditionary operations. The emphasis on joint and multinational cooperation has spawned multilevel joint, multinational, and Service military structures that interrelate horizontally and vertically. These organizations provide Marine Corps operational logisticians choices for sourcing resources. The MARFOR is at the center of converging chains of command, levels of war, and lateral relationships.

Marine Corps Forces

The Marine Corps either assigned or designated a MARFOR for each of the five unified combatant commands. The MARFOR is responsible for providing administrative and logistic support to the Marine Corps operating forces. Table 2-1 lists the unified combatant commands and their subordinate MARFOR.

Commander, Marine Corps Forces, Pacific

Figure 2-1 on page 2-2 shows the forces under COMMARFORPAC.

Commander, Marine Corps Forces, Atlantic

Figure 2-2 on page 2-3 shows the forces under COMMARFORLANT.

Logistic Authority and Support Arrangements

Understanding the different source documents that direct common-user logistics (CUL) and the

Table 2-1. Combatant Commands and Subordinate MARFOR.

Geographic Combatant Command	Relation-ship	Subordinate MARFOR
Commander in Chief, United States Pacific Command	Assigned*	Commander, Marine Corps Forces, Pacific (COMMARFORPAC)
Commander in Chief, United States Joint Forces Command	Assigned	Commander, Marine Corps Forces, Atlantic (COMMARFORLANT)
Commander in Chief, United States Central Command	Designated	Commander, Marine Corps Forces, Central Command
United States Commander in Chief, Europe	Assigned	Commander, Marine Corps Forces, Europe (COMMARFOREUR)
Commander in Chief, United States Southern Command	Designated	Commander, Marine Corps Forces, Southern Command

*Only the Secretary of Defense can assign or attach a force to a combatant command, and a force can only be assigned to one combatant command.

tools to facilitate common support is essential to understanding theater logistics external to the Marine Corps.

Sources

These sources include DOD executive agent directives and instructions, inter-Service and intra-governmental support agreements, acquisition and cross-Service agreements, and joint publications (JPs) (e.g., JP 0-2, *Unified Action Armed Forces [UNAAF]*; JP 4-0, *Doctrine for Logistic Support of Joint Operations*), and JFC operation plans (OPLANs)/operation orders (OPORDs) and directives.

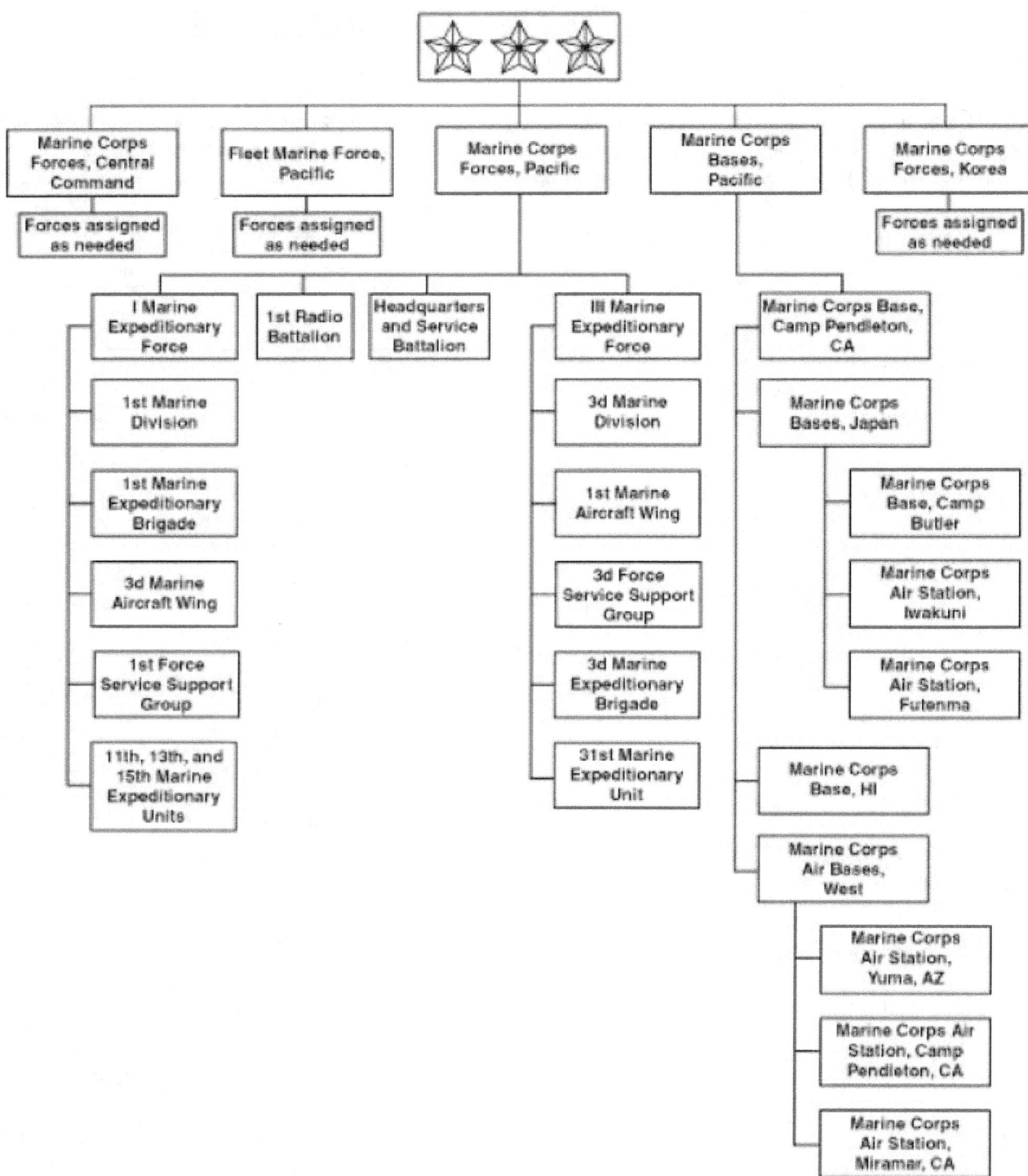

Figure 2-1. MARFOR Pacific, Central Command, and Korea.

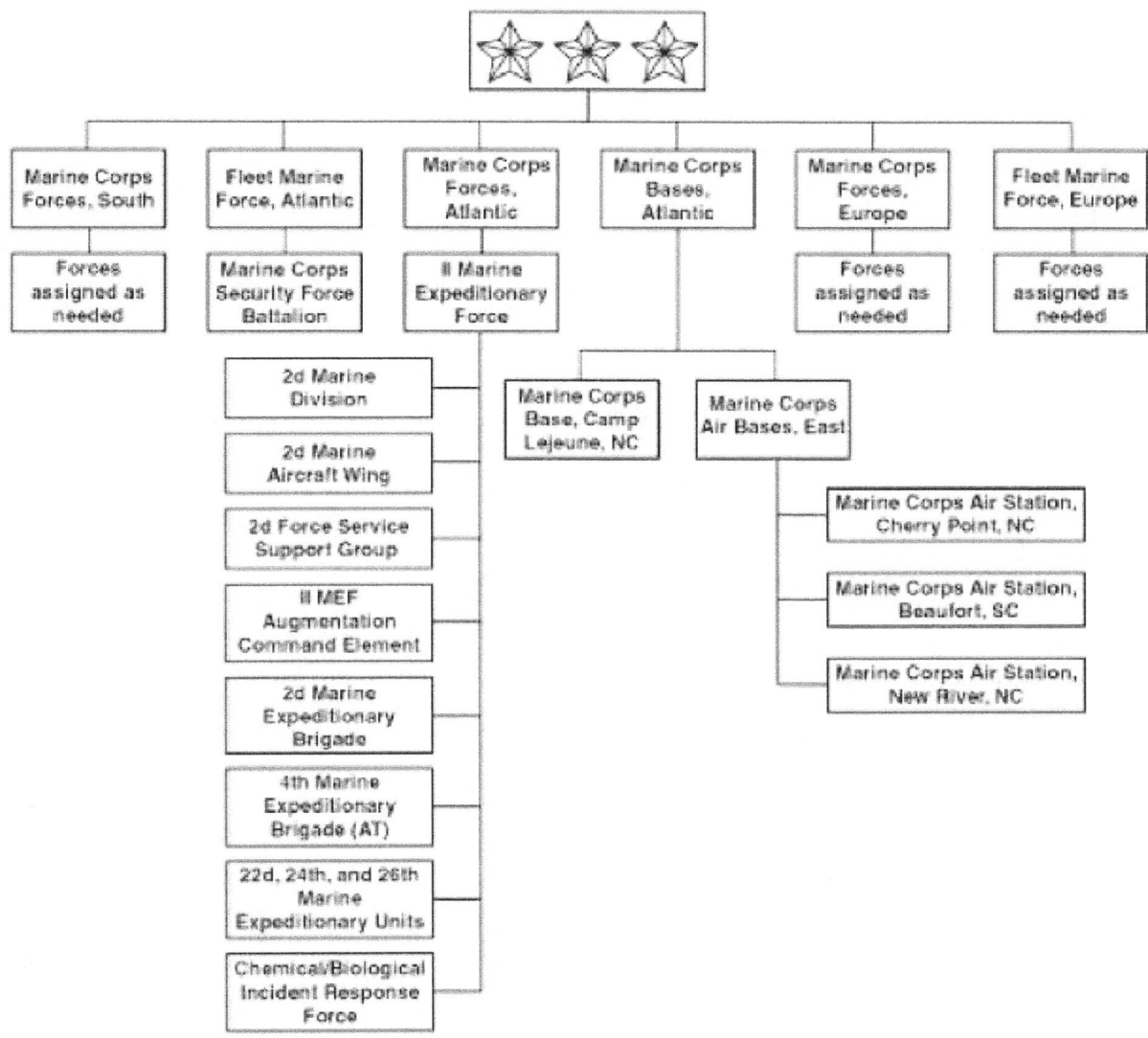

Figure 2-2. MARFOR Atlantic, Europe, and South.

DOD Executive Agent Directives and Instructions

The President, DOD, or Congress designates a DOD executive agent as the sole agency to perform a function or service for others. DOD executive agent responsibilities are normally focused on national strategic-level activities, but these responsibilities may also include operational-level logistic support in a theater of operations. Executive agent authority can be delegated by any superior to a subordinate to act on behalf of the superior. A wide range of responsibilities and authority may be given to the executive agent. The exact nature and scope of the authority delegated must be stated in the document designating the executive agent.

Inter-Service Support Agreement and Interdepartmental/Agency Support Agreements

Inter-Service support agreements are formal support agreements between two Services, or an element thereof, for one Service to provide logistic and/or administrative support to another. Such action may or may not be recurring on an installation, area or worldwide basis. Interdepartmental/agency support is the provision of logistic and/or administrative support services or materiel provided, with or without reimbursement, by one or more Services to one or more departments or agencies of the United States Government (other than military).

Acquisition Cross-Service Agreement

Negotiated on a bilateral basis with U.S. allies or coalition partners, acquisition cross-Service agreements (ACSAs) allow U.S. Forces to exchange common types of support (e.g., food, fuel, transportation, ammunition, equipment). ACSAs are bilateral agreements between the United States and one other nation or country. The support received or given is reimbursed under the ACSA through payment, replacement in kind or equal value exchange.

Support Relationships

CUL is materiel, items or service support shared with or provided by two or more Services, DOD agencies or multinational partners to another Service, DOD agency, non-DOD agency, and/or multinational partner in an operational environment. CUL performed by one Service in support of another Service may be in the form of—

- Common servicing that does not require reimbursement from the Service receiving the support.
- Cross-servicing that requires reimbursement from the Service receiving the support.

Marine Corps Support Organizations

The structural organization of the Marine Corps consists of HQMC, operating forces, the Marine Corps Reserve, and the SE. Each category has inherent logistic capabilities and specific logistic responsibilities at the strategic, operational, and tactical levels of war. The primary mission of HQMC and the SE is to provide manpower and logistic support to the operating forces. Responsibilities and capabilities overlap because no organization or level of support can function effectively without extensive, continuous coordination between supported and supporting organizations.

Headquarters, Marine Corps

Staffs, departments, and divisions of HQMC are responsible to the Commandant of the Marine Corps (CMC) for administrative management, policy, and provision of service support for the operating forces, the Marine Corps Reserve, and the SE. CMC delegates authority for designated matters of Marine Corps logistic policy and management to the Deputy Commandant for Installations and Logistics (I&L). This authority includes liaison and coordination for logistic action with HQMC staff principals, Marine Corps commanders, sister-Services, the joint staff, and DOD agencies. Responsible for designated aviation-specific logistic policy and management, the Deputy Commandant for Aviation coordinates logistic action with other agencies.

Supporting Establishment

The Marine Corps SE is responsible for manning and equipping the operating forces and is the source of Marine Corps strategic logistics. The Marine Corps SE consists of bases, stations, training activities, formal schools, the Marine Corps Recruiting Command, the Marine Corps Combat Development Command, and the Marine Corps Materiel Command (MARCORMATCOM).

Marine Corps Materiel Command

MARCORMATCOM has responsibility for materiel life cycle management of Marine Corps ground weapons systems, equipment, munitions, and information systems. This SE exercises materiel support management through its two subordinate commands, Marine Corps logistics bases (MCLBs) and Marine Corps Systems Command

(MARCORSYSCOM). The Marine Corps executes its supply functions via wholesale and retail material management entities. At the wholesale level, MCLBs perform traditional DOD inventory control point functions for assigned items, as well as serving as the single Service-level manager for Marine Corps ground weapons systems. At the retail level, MEFs operate intermediate stock points and process requisitions generated by the consumer-level maintenance and supply systems. The supply battalions of the force service support groups (FSSGs) operate these stock points and provide the primary source of supply for MEFs. The Navy provides support for Navy-furnished material, ammunition, and equipment through cognizant systems commands.

Marine Corps Logistics Bases

The MCLB, Albany, GA, MCLB Barstow, CA, and Blount Island Command (BIC), Jacksonville, FL, provide general Service-level supply, storage, and maintenance support to the Marine Corps. Repair centers perform depot-level overflow field/intermediate-level maintenance on ground equipment. Storage facilities house consumable and repairable materiel, including some pre-positioned war reserve materiel. MCLB Albany is the item manager for Marine Corps-peculiar materiel. BIC is responsible for inventory management and equipment maintenance, modification, and replacement support for the MPF and the Norway Geoprepositioning Program. MCLBs/BIC may deploy a technical assistance advisory team (TAAT), which includes civilian contractors, to a theater of war to provide technical assistance for MPF regeneration operations.

Marine Corps Systems Command

As one of its functions, the MARCORSYSCOM manages Marine Corps ground ammunition acquisition programs and Marine Corps owned and controlled ground ammunition stocks. The ground ammunition function is particularly significant in insuring MAGTF sustainability dur-

ing operations and crisis action response planning and execution.

Marine Corps Bases and Stations

Marine Corps bases, stations, and reserve support centers furnish the garrison administration, housing, storage, maintenance, training, and deployment support facilities. The operating forces and the Marine Corps Reserve use bases, stations, and centers to maintain their combat readiness and support their deployment on routine and contingency response operations. Bases, stations, and centers provide critical logistics to deploying forces during predeployment preparations. Many of the bases and stations of the SE report to either COMMARFORLANT or COMMARFORPAC. Some bases and stations are designated stations of initial assignment for Marine Corps Reserve mobilization and are responsible for assisting the operating forces with the throughput of Marine Corps Reserve personnel and materiel in support of MAGTF deployments.

Marine Corps Forces Logistic Sources

The MARFOR constitutes the forward presence, crisis response, and fighting power available to JFCs. The MAGTF, MLC, and the force projection logistic sources provide logistics for MARFOR.

Marine Air-Ground Task Force

The MAGTF is the principal Marine Corps organization for missions across the range of military operations. Task-organized under a single commander capable of responding rapidly anywhere in the world, MAGTF forces are functionally grouped into four elements: a command element (CE), an aviation combat element (ACE), a ground combat element (GCE), and a CSSE. The elements are categories of forces, not formal commands.

The basic MAGTF structure does not vary, though the number, size, and type units comprising each element will be mission dependent. The flexibility of the organizational structure allows for one or more subordinate MAGTFs, other Service, and/or foreign military forces to be assigned or attached. The MAGTF is specifically designed to meet mission-oriented requirements of amphibious warfare and expeditionary operations. A MAGTF deploys with a package of accompanying supplies that sustain initial operations. Though not part of the tactical command of the MAGTF, the SE provides the essential platform from which the MAGTF forms, trains, deploys, and receives sustainment.

Marine Expeditionary Force

The MEF is the largest MAGTF and the principal Marine Corps warfighting organization, particularly for larger crises or contingencies. It is task-organized around a permanent CE and normally contains one or more Marine divisions, Marine aircraft wings (MAWs), and Marine FSSGs. The MEF is capable of missions across the range of military operations, including amphibious assault and sustained operations ashore in any environment. It can operate from a sea base, a land base, or both. It may also contain other Service or foreign military forces assigned or attached to the MAGTF. The FSSG provides tactical-level ground CSS to MEF elements. The Marine wing support group (MWSG) provides aviation ground support, including airfield operations support and selected airfield-critical CSS functions to the MAW and to Marine aircraft groups (MAGs) through the Marine wing support squadron (MWSS). Marine aviation logistics squadrons (MALSs) provide direct intermediate-level aviation supply, maintenance, avionics, and ordnance support to a MAG.

The MEF deploys with up to 60 days of accompanying supplies. Under certain conditions, a MEF operating in a joint force may receive operational-level logistics from an FSSG designated as an MLC. Smaller MAGTFs are task-organized from the assets of the MEF.

Marine Expeditionary Brigade

A Marine expeditionary brigade (MEB) is a MAGTF that is constructed around a reinforced infantry regiment, a composite MAG, and a brigade service support group (BSSG). Commanded by a general officer, the MEB is task-organized to meet the requirements of a specific situation. It can function as part of a joint task force (JTF), as the lead echelon of the MEF, or alone. Varying in size and composition, the MEB is larger than a Marine expeditionary unit (MEU) but smaller than a MEF. The MEB is capable of conducting missions across the full range of military operations. It may contain other Service or foreign military forces assigned or attached. As an expeditionary force, the MEB is capable of rapid deployment and employment with maritime or geographic pre-positioning equipment and supplies via amphibious shipping and/or strategic airlift. A MEB normally deploys with up to 30 days of accompanying supplies.

Marine Expeditionary Unit

A MEU is a MAGTF that is constructed around an infantry battalion reinforced, a helicopter squadron reinforced, and a MEU service support group (MSSG). It normally fulfills Marine Corps forward sea-based deployment requirements. The MEU provides an immediate reaction capability for crisis response and is capable of limited combat operations. It may contain other Service or foreign military forces assigned or attached. The MSSG is sourced from an FSSG. The standard accompanying sustainment for a MEU is up to 15 days of accompanying supplies.

Special Purpose MAGTF

A special purpose Marine air-ground task force (SPMAGTF) is a MAGTF organized, trained, and equipped with narrowly focused capabilities. It is designed to accomplish a specific mission, often of limited scope and duration. A SPMAGTF may be any size, but normally it is a relatively small force—the size of a MEU or smaller. It may contain other Service or foreign military forces assigned or attached to the MAGTF. Normally, a combat service support detachment (CSSD) is task-organized from the FSSG to support the SPMAGTF. When attached to a joint force, the SPMAGTF will usually require operational logistic support.

Air Contingency MAGTF

The air contingency MAGTF (ACM) is an on-call, combat-ready MAGTF that deploys by airlift. ACMs vary in size based on mission requirements and the availability of airlift. Because they deploy by air, ACMs generally have a limited organic logistics capability, require an arrival airfield, and need operational logistic support. ACMs usually are activated to respond to developing crises and may deploy independently or in conjunction with other expeditionary forces.

Marine Logistics Command

The MLC is an employment option available to the Marine Corps component commander for executing operational logistics and is the primary option to provide operational-level support during a major theater war (MTW). The MLC is the Marine Corps logistic organization that fills the gap between the tactical and strategic levels of logistics. The MLC is task-organized around a BSSG/combat service support group (CSSG) or larger CSSE to provide operational logistic support to theater MARFOR, including MAGTFs operating with the Navy component. The MLC normally falls under the U.S. chain of command and provides U.S. logistic support; however, as directed by the CINC, the MLC may provide CUL to multinational and joint forces.

The MLC is the MARFOR's operational-level logistic agency to coordinate host nation, joint, and coalition support and to execute the MARFOR commander's logistic policy. When a CSSE is designated as the MLC, the MARFOR establishes the support relationship between the MLC and the MAGTF. The establishment of an MLC creates an operational/tactical logistic structure within the Marine Corps component where one CSSE serving as an MLC is normally responsible for operational-level logistics, and the MAGTF CSSE is responsible for the CSS of the MAGTF.

The MLC is attached to the component command (see figure 2-3) and has coordinating authority with supported MAGTFs. The MLC and FSSG commanders exercise C2 of their assigned organizations by structuring their forces, establishing command relationships, and assigning missions to meet changing requirements.

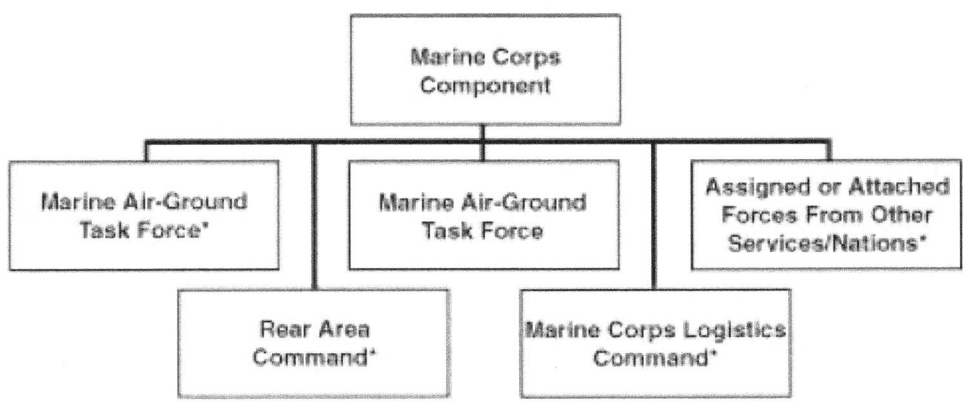

*As required or assigned.

Figure 2-3. MLC in a Marine Corps Component Organization.

Force Projection Logistic Sources

To respond rapidly to crises in different parts of the world, the Marine Corps and the Navy developed the MPF and aviation logistics support ship (T-AVB) programs. In concert with NATO and the Norwegians, the Marine Corps maintains the Norway Geoprepositioning Program as another logistic source.

Maritime Pre-positioning Force

The MPF is a highly responsive, strategic power projection capability that currently consists of 15 ships organized into 3 maritime pre-positioning ships squadrons (MPSRONs). These squadrons are strategically positioned around the world and are loaded with the equipment and supplies to sustain a notional 17,600-member force for up to 30 days. A MEB will enter a theater of operations via air or sealift and join the equipment and supplies unloaded at a nearby port during arrival and assembly operations.

An MPF consists of a MEB, ships of the MPSRON, and Navy support forces. An MPSRON can also support smaller MAGTFs through selective offloading of equipment and supplies or a MEF by employing some or all of the 15 ships. Ships from one MPSRON are interchangeable with ships from any other. MPF is especially responsive to regional crises or natural disaster relief. Each squadron flagship and alternate flagship is configured to support a MEU-size contingency, which allows for the download of a MEU suite of equipment and sustainment by one ship.

MPF and amphibious operations are complementary capabilities; one is not a substitute for the other. MPF is not to be confused with JLOTS, strategic sealift, or a floating warehouse. Such inappropriate use of equipment and supplies degrades MPF capability and could jeopardize the combatant commander's ability to employ MAGTFs.

Aviation Logistics Support Ship

There are two T-AVBs, one located on the West Coast and the other on the East Coast. They provide dedicated sealift for movement of MALS supplies and equipment, and they provide an intermediate maintenance activity aboard ship. This immediate maintenance activity is task-organized to repair aircraft parts and equipment for MAGTF aircraft.

Norway Geoprepositioning Program

Established in 1981 under a bilateral memorandum of understanding with the Norwegian Government, this program permits the pre-positioning and maintenance of MEB equipment and supplies in underground storage facilities in Norway. The equipment and supplies are categorized as contingency retention stock. Since 1995, the two countries have equally shared the cost of the program. The Norway Geoprepositioning Program provides the Norway air-landed Marine expeditionary brigade (NALMEB) a capability similar in scope to that of an MPSRON.

The NALMEB, totaling approximately 13,000 personnel, is smaller than a maritime pre-positioning ship (MPS) MEB. Similarly, the NALMEB does not pre-position armor assets due to Norway's non-provocation policy and the Conventional Forces in Europe Treaty. HQMC approved the use of equipment and supplies for exercises or operations outside of Norway but within the European Command area of responsibility (AOR). The NALMEB Out of Area Policy allows for this by requesting the use of these assets from HQMC via the appropriate chain of command/national command relationships. HQMC has designated COMMARFOREUR as its executive agent for these matters once HQMC approval has been granted. Requests for exception to this policy must be forwarded to HQMC for approval.

Joint Force Logistic Organizations

Combatant commanders and subordinate JFCs rely on a variety of organizations to coordinate logistic activities within the joint force. The J-4 is the primary coordinating staff agency in the joint force and usually forms a logistics readiness center (LRC) to monitor events in theater. Additionally, the JFC has the option of establishing numerous logistic offices, boards, and centers to coordinate theater logistics.

Logistics Division

The logistics division is charged with the formulation of logistic plans and with the coordination and supervision of supply, maintenance, repair, evacuation, transportation, engineering, salvage, procurement, health services, mortuary affairs, communications system support, security assistance, host-nation support (HNS), and related logistic activities. Because many of the problems confronting this division are of a single-Service nature, the established policies of the Service should be considered. This division is responsible for advising the commander of the logistic support that can be provided for proposed courses of action (COAs). In general, the J-4 formulates policies to ensure effective logistic support for forces in the command and coordinates execution of the commander's policies and guidance. The joint forces logistic staff performs the following functions:

- Monitors current and evolving theater logistic capabilities.
- Coordinates logistics with upcoming operations.
- Advises the JFC on the supportability of proposed operations and COAs.
- Acts as agent and advocate to non-theater logistic organizations.

Logistics Readiness Center

The J-4 may establish an LRC to monitor events within theater. The LRC receives reports from Service components and external sources, distills information for presentation to the JFC, and responds to questions. The LRC consists of representatives from various functional areas (e.g., fuels, ammunition, engineering, supply, surface transportation, sealift, airlift, medical services). The LRC performs the following tasks:

- Plans for and monitors current and evolving theater logistic capabilities.
- Directs and coordinates logistic support with upcoming operations.
- Advises the JFC on the supportability of proposed operations or COA.
- Monitors logistic automation systems for asset status.
- Acts as the JFC's agent and advocate to non-theater logistic organizations.

Logistic Offices, Boards, and Centers

Combatant commanders or subordinate JFC may establish joint logistic offices, boards, and centers, to coordinate logistics.

Joint Petroleum Office

The Joint Petroleum Office (JPO) supervises the combatant commander's fuels responsibility within a theater. In conjunction with the Service components and the defense energy support center (DESC), the JPO plans, coordinates, and oversees bulk petroleum support for U.S. Forces employed or planned for employment in the theater. A field activity of DLA, DESC is the integrated materiel manager for bulk petroleum. When tactical operations warrant extensive management of wholesale bulk petroleum, the JPO may establish a sub-area petroleum office (SAPO).

Sub-area Petroleum Office

The primary function of the SAPO is to supervise the staff petroleum logistic responsibilities of a joint force. The Service component commander augments the SAPO with personnel to perform the following tasks within the AOR:

- Reviews and consolidates resupply requirements for JPO and DESC.

- Releases or reallocates pre-positioned war reserve materiel stocks.
- Assists the DESC.
- Identifies and submits requirements to host nation(s) for petroleum logistic support.

Joint Civil-Military Engineering Board

The joint civil-military engineering board (JCMEB) establishes in-theater policies, procedures, priorities, and direction for civil-military construction and engineering requirements. The JCMEB is a temporary board staffed by personnel from the components, agencies or activities. The JCMEB arbitrates issues referred by the Joint Facilities Utilization Board (JFUB) and, if appropriate, prepares the civil engineering support plan.

Joint Facilities Utilization Board

The JFUB evaluates and reconciles component requests for real estate, use of existing facilities, inter-Service support, and construction to comply with JCMEB priorities. The J-4 chairs the JFUB, whose membership includes representatives from the components and special activities (e.g., legal and civil affairs).

CINC Logistic Procurement Support Board

The CINC logistic procurement support board (CLPSB) coordinates the JFC's theater acquisition program. A J-4 representative chairs the CLPSB, which is staffed by representatives from each component. The CLPSB performs the following functions:

- Coordinates the acquisition of supplies and services performed under U.S. contracts with U.S. Embassies and host nation(s).
- Assigns single-Service contracting for specified supplies and services, when appropriate.
- Exchanges information between contracting activities addressing sources of supply, prices, contractor performance, etc.
- Provides guidance on the consolidation of purchases.

- Establishes procedures to coordinate procurement with the supply operations.
- Prescribes payment procedures consistent with currency-control requirements and international agreements.
- Promulgates classification and compensation guides governing wages, living allowances, and other benefits for third world country national and indigenous employees.

Theater Patient Movement Requirements Center

The JFS controls the theater patient movement requirements center (TPMRC), which coordinates and controls the inter/intratheater movement of patients. The TPMRC generates theater plans and schedules that deliver patients to medical treatment facilities (MTFs).

Joint Blood Program Office

The Joint Blood Program Office (JBPO) plans, coordinates, and directs the handling, storage, and distribution of blood and blood components within the AOR. The JBPO consolidates and forwards requirements for resupply to the Armed Services Blood Program Office (ASBPO). The JBPO functions within the office of the JFS and is staffed with Service representatives knowledgeable in blood bank techniques.

Joint Mortuary Affairs Office

The joint mortuary affairs office (JMAO) plans and executes mortuary affairs programs. The JMAO provides guidance to facilitate the conduct of mortuary programs and to maintain data (as required) pertaining to recovery, identification, and disposition of U.S. dead and missing in the assigned theater. The JMAO serves as the central clearing point for mortuary affairs and casualty information, and monitors the deceased and missing personal effects program. The Army component commander is routinely designated executive agent for theater mortuary affairs, which includes the establishment and operation of the JMAO under the staff supervision of a JFC J-4.

Joint Medical Surveillance Team

The joint medical surveillance team is responsible for the following:

● Coordinates, monitors, and evaluates the health surveillance activities of force health protection in support of joint operations.

● Provides the clinical and administrative expertise to ensure compliance with health surveillance policies and programs and maintains the highest level of accountability.

● Ensures proper documentation of health surveillance initiatives, to include pre- and post-deployment questionnaires, serum samples, immunizations, disease and non-battle injury reports, and environmental samples.

● Assists in the risk communication and health education and training program.

● Collects and analyzes medical threat and health surveillance data.

● Recommends intervention strategies for minimizing casualties and optimizing health readiness.

● Documents lessons learned for improving the health surveillance program in subsequent operations.

Joint Materiel Priorities and Allocation Board

The Joint Materiel Priorities and Allocation Board recommends priorities for allocations of materiel to fulfill in-theater logistic requirements for both U.S. and allied forces.

Joint Transportation Board

The combatant command establishes a JTB to establish priorities and allocations of common-user transportation resources within the CINC's geographic region.

Joint Movement Center

The JMC is responsible for coordinating the employment of all modes of theater transportation (i.e., allies, coalition partners or the host nation) to support the theater concept of operations. The JMC establishes strategic and theater transportation policies consistent with relative urgency of need, port and terminal capabilities, transportation asset availability, and the JFC's priorities. The functions and responsibilities of the JMC are theater-dependent.

Service and Civilian Components

Joint policy encourages the Service components to coordinate, consult, and agree on common procedures for efficient utilization of logistic resources. In addition, the combatant commander may exercise directive authority for logistics (DAL) and direct a single Service to provide common-user support to the joint force. Operational-level logistic planners must be familiar with other Service capabilities to maximize the use of available theater resources and create the conditions for MAGTF success.

Navy

The Navy component command (NCC) is responsible for the preparing and equipping of Navy forces needed for the effective prosecution of war and other military operations.

Capabilities

Table 2-2 on page 2-12 lists Navy logistic units and functions performed by the NCC.

Table 2-2. NCC Operational-Level Logistic Capabilities.

Type Unit	Functions
Naval cargo handling battalions	Organizing, training, and equipping to load and off-load Navy and Marine Corps cargo in MPF and merchant breakbulk or container ships; operating a temporary ocean cargo terminal; loading and offloading cargo carrier in military-controlled aircraft; and operating an expeditionary air cargo terminal.
Freight terminal companies	Forwarding cargo at seaports.
Fixed-wing and rotary-wing squadrons	Distributing cargo and passengers in-theater.
Naval supply support battalions	Supply support warehousing (e.g., inventory management, asset visibility).
Naval facilities engineering command, Atlantic and Pacific divisions	Contingency engineering, constructing facilities, and providing services contracting as well as engineering and environmental technical support.
Naval construction force (NCF) units, including NMCBs, amphibious construction battalions, and underwater construction teams. (These NCF engineering forces are referred to as SEABEEs.)	Constructing and maintaining facilities and lines of communications (LOCs), constructing port facilities and erecting causeway and elevated causeway systems in support of JLOTS.
Fleet hospitals, hospital ships, and casualty receiving and treatment ships (CRTSs) mobile medical augmentation readiness team and fleet surgical teams	Providing HSS.
Service support elements, naval regional contracting centers	Providing mobile mail centers, contracting support for CSS (e.g., messing, berthing, finance, laundry, barber, retail outlet, transportation).
Fuel companies	Storing and distributing bulk fuel, providing tank trucks, operating fuel service stations operations, limiting pollution, and providing environmental clean up.

Elements

The logistics task force (LTF) and combat logistics force (CLF) are elements of the Navy theater distribution organization.

Logistics Task Force. An LTF is responsible for recommending, planning, and sourcing expeditionary logistic support to each of the combatant commander's Navy component commanders.

Combat Logistics Force. The CLF provides underway replenishment to battle groups, amphibious-ready groups, embarked units, and individual ships at sea. Highly mobile, the CLF carries a broad range of stores (e.g., fuel, food, repair parts, ammunition, other essential materiel) to keep the naval forces operating at sea for extended periods. The CLF consists of station ships, shuttle ships, and a variety of other support ships. It includes both active Navy ships and those operated by the MSC within the naval fleet auxiliary force. Shore-based naval logistics introduces additional planning requirements. Sites must be identified to establish the following capabilities:

- Naval advanced logistic support site (ALSS) and naval forward logistic site (FLS). The shore-based system theater distribution of the Navy is based on an ALSS located near major transportation terminals and FLSs forward-positioned to support Navy forces. The ALSS/FLS receive, consolidate, stow, and transfer supplies and equipment to shore-based aviation units, fleet hospitals, NMCBs, and other Navy units operating on land as well as to Navy operating forces afloat.

- Advanced base functional components (ABFCs) are task-organized equipment and/or personnel modules that conduct or augment the shore-based logistic operations of the ALSS and FLSs. Each ABFC performs specific logistic functions that may be combined to establish or extend the shore-based infrastructure. ABFCs may be sourced from any combination of reserve or active forces and contracted support.

Army

The Army Service Component Command (ASCC) is an Army component to the geographical combatant commanders and the major sub-unified command. The ASCCs are responsible for the preparation of Army forces (ARFOR) necessary for the effective prosecution of war and other military operations. The ASCC routinely plans for and provides the following theater logistic functions:

- Management of overland petroleum support including inland waterways to U.S. land-based forces of DOD components.
- Common item and common service support to other components as required by the combatant commander.
- Theater land LOC.
- Common-user land transportation in theater to include rail.
- Equipment load-rigging support in conjunction with other Service component commands.
- In-theater water terminal operations in coordination with the Military Traffic Management Command (MTMC) port manager.
- Pipeline fuel support.
- Establishment and operation of inland waterways and coastal barge traffic in conjunction with MTMC.
- Engineer support for the inland distribution network (i.e., highways and bridges).
- Rotary-wing, common-user support, especially in the area of medical evacuation.
- Logistic support to allied/coalition commands and/or interagency support for specific support, as directed by the combatant commander.

Lead Service Common-User Logistics

Each Service component to a JFC is responsible for the personnel and logistic support of its own subordinate forces, except when this support is otherwise provided for by agreements with other Services, DOD agencies, multinational partners, or by assignments of common support require-

ments by the JFC. CUL requirements within unified operations can be short or long term. These requirements are the ASCC commander's responsibility, although they may be executed by tactical-level ARFOR support headquarters. CUL requirements can come from numerous sources. These sources include formal DOD-level executive agent responsibilities, inter-Service support agreements, support agreements between U.S. Forces and allies and lead-Service designation as determined by the combatant commander. CUL is discussed further in JP 4-07, *Joint Tactics, Techniques, and Procedures for Common-User Logistic Support During Joint Operation.*

Elements

The Army has numerous operational logistic organizations (echelons above corps [EAC]) and one tactical organization that may provide theater-level logistic support.

Theater Support Command

The theater support command (TSC) is a multifunctional support headquarters that works at the operational level with links to strategic- and tactical-level support organizations and agencies. The ASCC commander supervises the TSC's peacetime contingency planning. When deploying to an AO, the TSC reports to the commander, Army forces (COMARFOR). The COMARFOR may be the ASCC commander or a lower level commander, depending on the scale of operations. The TSC has some permanently assigned major subordinate units. The centerpiece of the TSC is the distribution management center (DMC), which combines the functions of materiel management and movement. The logistics support element (LSE) and area support groups (ASGs) are subordinate elements of the TSC. The ASCC commander attaches other units to the TSC for specific operations. The TSC can be easily tailored to best meet the support requirements that can vary considerably depending on the type of operations and the scale of the deployment.

In many operational scenarios, the TSC commander would execute most of COMARFOR's lead Service CUL responsibilities in the AO. TSC planners must be aware of the support responsibilities falling to other Army EAC-level commands and synchronize it with any applicable portion of the distribution plan.

The Army normally executes movement control for EAC at the operational level through a TSC movement control agency (MCA). In some instances, this organization reports to the primary logistics staff officer in the ASCC staff. The TSC MCA helps develop and executes the Army posture of the joint movement program developed by the JMC.

The TSC MCA serves as the primary element for the planning and controlling of transportation operations at the operational level. The TSC MCA synchronizes its operations with those of the JMC, USTRANSCOM, the TSC DMC, and lower echelon MCCs. It also follows the priorities established by the ASCC.

At the operational level, the TSC's maintenance capability is organized to provide DS and GS maintenance to units in and passing through the AO, to provide DS maintenance support to back up tactical-level organizations, support to aviation units, and sustainment maintenance support for the theater. The support operations supply and maintenance directorate provides planning and policy for maintenance provided by Army maintenance units, maintenance elements under the LSE, and contracted support.

The TSC manages Class I, II, III (packaged and bulk), IV, V, VI, VII, and IX supplies and water. Class IV supply actions are coordinated with the engineer command and/or COMARFOR engineer staff. The TSC director of field services exercises staff supervision over field services functions. ARFOR, via the TSC, may be responsible to provide significant field service CUL support within the AO/joint operations area (JOA).

The Army developed a modular concept for opening theaters in which the TSC is a critical component. Modularity involves incrementally deploying only the minimum capabilities required to an AO, and the basis for this modular support is called the theater force opening package. The TSC early entry module provides C2 of many of the elements initially supporting RSOI.

Logistics Support Element

The LSE is a forward deployed theater-specific organization that performs the United States Army Materiel Command (USAMC) tasks of depot maintenance, oil analysis, calibration of test equipment, ammunition surveillance, release of pre-positioned strategic stocks, materiel fielding, technology insertion, and battle damage assessment. USAMC staffs the LSE headquarters while a combination of DOD civilians, contractors, military, and host-nation personnel augment the operational units of the organization. The LSE is operational control (OPCON) to the TSC.

Area Support Group

ASGs, subordinate units assigned to the TSC, are responsible for area support in the AO and may be tasked to provide sustainment support to Marine Corps or other forces. The basic mission of the ASG is to provide DS logistics support to designated units and elements within its AOR. This support typically includes DS supply (less ammunition, classified map supply, and medical supply and support), DS maintenance, field services, as well as other support directed by COMARFOR through the TSC. ASGs can also provide GS supply and sustainment maintenance support to TSC and combat-zone DS supply organizations and sustainment maintenance in support of the theater mission. If an operational-level ammunition group is not established, specialized battalions assigned to the ASG provide ammunition support. ASGs can support intermediate staging base and RSOI operations.

ASGs are composed of specialized and multifunctional units. The mission, functions, and organization of ASGs vary according to the type and extent of support required.

ASGs provide a wide variety of support to units stationed in or passing through their areas. An ASG area of support depends on the density of military units and materiel to be supported and on political boundaries and identifiable terrain features. Normally, one ASG is assigned to a TSC for every 15,000 to 30,000 troops supported in the AO. ASGs are generally located along land LOC to take advantage of the transportation network and to provide responsive support to the units they support.

Corps Support Command

The size and composition of the corps support command (COSCOM) depend on the type of Army corps (e.g. airborne, armored), number of soldiers to be supported, type of organizations supported, number and types of weapon systems to repair, and tonnage of supplies to be issued and transported. The COSCOM consists of a special troop battalion and headquarters company, functional control centers, a variable number of corps support groups (CSGs), a medical brigade, and a transportation group. COSCOMs are designed to provide tactical-level DS and GS support to corps units, but with proper staff and unit augmentation, COSCOMs can perform significant operational-level support functions.

Air Force

The commander, Air Force forces (COMAFFOR), consists of assigned combat and service aviation forces. The COMAFFOR is responsible for the preparation of the air forces to prosecute war effectively and other military missions. At the operational level of logistics, the COMAFFOR provides intratheater airlift, aerial port operations, and airdrop services to the joint force. It controls theater operations through the air operations center (AOC).

Director of Mobility Forces

The director of mobility forces (DIRMOBFOR) is normally a senior officer familiar with the JOA and possesses an extensive background in airlift operations. When established, DIRMOBFOR serves as the designated agent of the Air Force component commander or joint force air component commander for airlift issues. In addition, the DIRMOBFOR exercises coordinating authority between the airlift coordination cell, the air mobility element, the tanker airlift control center, the JMC, and the AOC to expedite the resolution of airlift problems.

Air Operations Center

The AOC is the principal air operations installation from which aircraft and air warning functions of combat air operations are directed, controlled, and executed. The AOC is the senior agency of the COMAFFOR from which C2 of air operations are coordinated with other components and Services.

Airlift Coordination Cell

An airlift coordination cell within the AOC plans, coordinates, manages, and executes theater airlift operations in the AOR or JOA. Normally, the air coordination cell consists of an airlift plans branch, an airlift operations branch, and an airlift support branch.

Aeromedical Evacuation Coordination Center

The aeromedical evacuation coordination center (AECC) is a coordination center, within the joint AOC's airlift coordination cell, that monitors aeromedical evacuation (AE) operations. The AECC manages the medical aspects of the AE mission and serves as the net control station for AE communications. It coordinates medical requirements with airlift capability, assigns medical missions to the appropriate AE elements, and monitors patient movement activities.

Air Force Contingency Supply Squadron

The Air Force contingency supply squadron (AFCSS) provides global supply, fuels, accounting, and supply computer support to the geographical combatant commanders or major air force command during wartime, contingency, natural disaster, or humanitarian relief operations. The level of support provided by the AFCSS depends on the situation and the support requested by the major command or the supported combatant commander. The AFCSS provides limited support for deployments less than 30 days. For operation greater than 30 days, the AFCSS provides full supply support to include funds management, stock control, and monitoring of requisitions, fuels accounting, and base operating support.

Civilian

The civilian augmentation program is a DOD program designed to use civilian contractors to perform selected services during military operations. Civilian contractors are used to displace deployed forces, allowing them to be redeployed for other contingencies and to limit the size of a military force in-theater.

Interagency Theater Organizations

Interagency organizations are DOD, other U.S. Government departments or agencies, NGOs, regional organizations, and international organizations. The MARFOR may join a number of interagency organizations in theater, especially during MOOTW.

Nongovernmental Organizations

NGOs are transnational organizations of private citizens that maintain a consultative status with the Economic and Social Council of the United Nations. NGOs may be professional associations, foundations, multinational businesses, or simply groups with a common interest in humanitarian assistance (development and relief). NGO is a term normally used by non-U.S. organizations. Examples are Doctors without Borders and Save the Children Fund.

The United Nations

The United Nations, Department of Peacekeeping Operations, Field and Logistics Division, Logistics and Communications Services is the logistic organization responsible for most United Nations operations. This organization plans logistic support, determines support requirements, participates in technical survey teams, manages and arranges deployments, and determines the need for construction projects.

Multinational Theater Organization

Multinational operations are conducted by coalitions or alliances between two or more nations and are initiated to achieve common interests. A coalition is an ad hoc arrangement between two or more nations for common action. An alliance is the result of formal agreements between two or more nations for broad, long-term objectives that further the common interests of the members. Multinational operations participants are generally reluctant to grant the multinational force commanders (MNFCs) full control over their forces.

Logistic Principles

Multinational logistics (MNL) is defined as any coordinating logistic activity involving two or more countries or organizations in support of MNFs. The following principles guide forces participating in MNL:

● Logistic support is a collective responsibility of the MNF and the participating nations.
● Individual nations are responsible for the logistic support of their forces.

- MNFC must have sufficient authority over logistic resources.
- Cooperation and coordination are necessary.
- Mutual support agreements reduce the logistic footprint in a theater.
- Synergy results from the use of multinational integrated logistic support.
- MNFC must have visibility of the logistic activities during an operation.

Logistic Structure

The MNF logistic structure is complex, but generally parallels the U.S. joint/Service structure. The purpose and operations of the multinational joint logistic center (MJLC) overlap and are based on the specific requirements of the operation. Table 2-3 shows joint/multinational/Service-level organizations.

Table 2-3. Joint/Multinational/Service-Level Organizations.

Level	Multinational	U.S. Joint/Service
Joint force	• MNFC senior theater logistician • MJLC	• J-4 • LRC • Joint logistic boards, offices, and centers
Component	Multinational logistic center (MNLC).	• National support element (NSE) • MLC
Operating forces	Multinational integrated logistic units (MILUs)	• NSEs • FSSG, BSSG, MWSG, MWSS

MNFC Senior Theater Logistician

The combined/joint logistics representative is the multinational equivalent of the J-4. The senior theater logistician develops initial logistical guidance, plans for the logistical support of the operation, and promulgates logistic policies on behalf of the MNFC. The senior theater logistician has the following responsibilities:

- Plans the logistic support necessary to support the MNFC's concept of operations.

- Identifies operational-level logistic force requirements to support the operation.
- Determines and establishes lead-nation responsibilities within the assigned AO.
- Determines host-nation/theater resource requirements/availability and negotiates necessary agreements.
- Assesses logistic strength of particular forces; identifies logistic shortfalls; and, in coordination with nation representatives, initiates actions necessary to remedy the shortfalls.
- Prioritizes logistic requirements in accordance with MNFC guidance and deconflicts competing requirements.
- Identifies common-funded requirements, develops budgets, and seeks appropriate funding.
- Establishes and publishes logistic reporting requirements.
- Establishes the MNL C2 organization, determines manning, and harmonizes unit rotation schedules with the needs of the MNF.
- Interfaces at the national level with those nations providing logistic assets/units for operations.
- Interfaces, as necessary, with the national contingents, especially with the host nations.
- Provides/implements logistic planning guidance in conjunction with the MNFC logistic planning staff.
- Coordinates the early development of logistic support plans to meet the needs of evolving operations.

Multinational Joint Logistic Center

The MJLC coordinates or controls the logistic activities of designated organizations to support the MNF. In addition, it operates functionally oriented centralized coordination centers.

Centralized Coordination Centers

These organizations are functional, under the command of the MJLC, and are roughly equivalent to the joint offices, boards, and centers. The MJLC activates centralized coordination centers for joint logistic operations, HNS/theater resources, theater allied contracting, medical coordination center (MEDCC), theater movement coordination center (TMCC), engineering, and others as needed. These centers coordinate logistics with the MNLC.

Multinational Logistic Centers

MNLCs coordinate logistics at the national Service component level, such as the MARFOR.

Multinational Integrated Logistic Units

MILUs are organized when two or more nations agree to provide logistic assets to an MNF. The MILU is OPCON to either the MNFC or a national Service component commander.

National Support Element

NSEs are national organizations or activities that support national forces attached to a MNF. NSEs are OPCON to national authorities and are not normally part of the MNF. Their mission is nation-specific support to units and common support that is retained by the nation. NSEs coordinate and cooperate with the host-nation commander and the host nation. The MLC, FSSG, BSSG, MWSG, and MWSS are examples of NSEs.

CHAPTER 3. COMMAND AND CONTROL

Operational logistic C2 involves the organizations, communications, and processes needed to generate, collect, and transmit the necessary logistic information to execute force closure, sustainment, and reconstitution and redeployment. Logistic C2 has three primary goals—recognizing needed support and ensuring the support reaches units that need it, anticipating future requirements, and allocating resources. C2 supports the operational logistic planning, decision, execution, and assessment (PDE&A) cycle. It enables the component commander to exchange logistic information with joint, multinational, other Service components, host nation, the MAGTF, and the strategic base. The operational logistics C2 begins with the national military command structure.

National Military Command Structure

Marine Corps combatant command-level components occupy a point of convergence between the operational and Service (administrative) chains of command in the national military command structure. See figure 3-1. Below the National Command Authorities (NCA), the two chains of command diverge with the operational chain running through

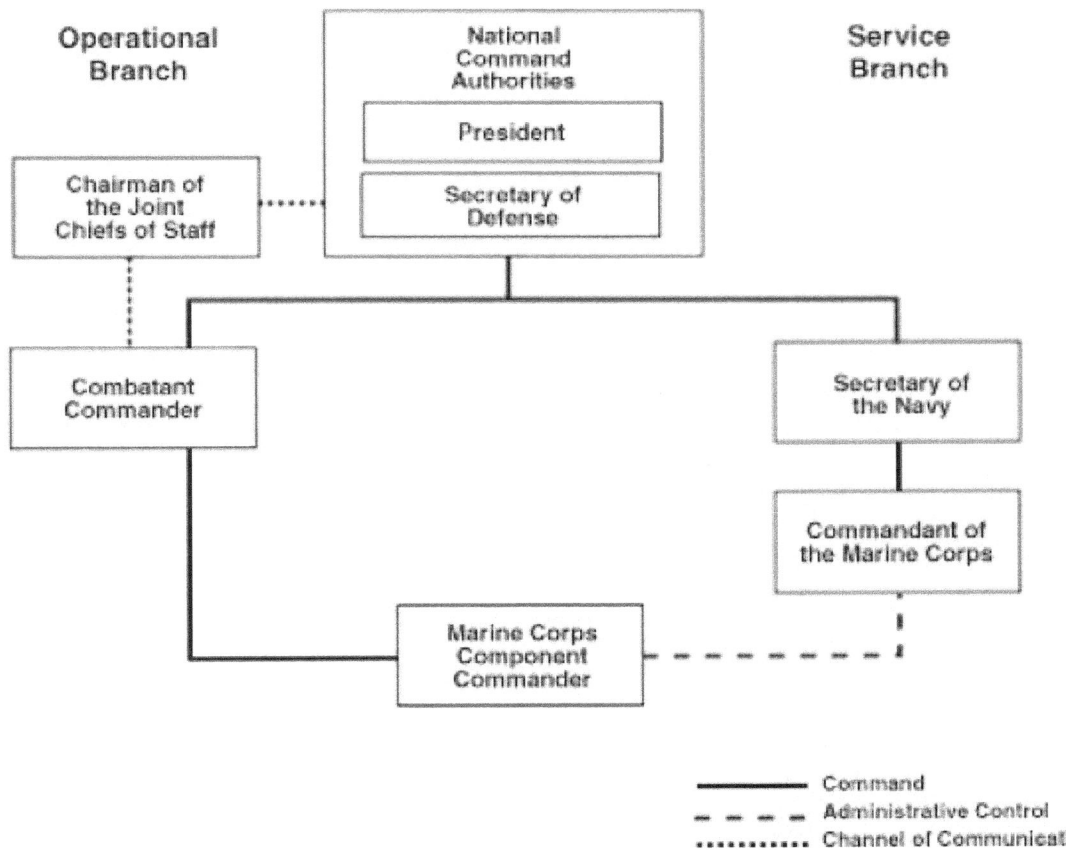

Figure 3-1. Chain of Command.

the combatant commands to the Service component and with administrative authority flowing through the Service secretaries and Service chiefs to the Service component commander.

Joint Forces

There are three levels of joint forces: unified commands, subordinate unified commands, and JTFs. The NCA has established nine unified commands, also referred to as CINCs, to perform broad continuing missions. The five combatant commands are responsible for a geographical area, while the unified commands are functionally responsible for transportation, space, special operations, and strategic forces. The CINC, United States Transportation Command (USCINCTRANS) is the functional unified commander for transportation.

Combatant commanders may form standing subordinate unified commands to perform broad and continuing missions. For limited and temporary operations, JTFs are established that report to either a combatant command, subordinate unified command, or an existing JTF. COMMARFORPAC can establish and deploy two JTF headquarters, and COMMARFORLANT can deploy one JTF headquarters, ordered by their combatant commanders.

Joint commanders organize their commands either by function, Service component, or by a combination of both methods. Joint forces with assigned and/or attached MARFOR have Marine Corps Service components.

Marine Corps Components

The Marine Corps has three methods of organizing and staffing the two levels of componency shown in table 3-1.

A combatant command-level MARFOR is formed on a continuing basis. The combatant-level commander, Marine Corps forces (COMMARFOR) may deploy with a staff in situations where the CINC and principal staff deploy to the operational area. When deployed to a theater of war, the MARFOR can be organized with two commanders and two staffs or with one commander and two staffs.

Two-Commanders/Two-Staff Method

In the two-commander/two-staff arrangement, one commander and one staff function as the MARFOR, while the other commander, supported by a staff, commands the MAGTF.

One-Commander/Two-Staff Method

In the one-commander/two-staff arrangement, one commander is dual-hatted as COMMARFOR and MAGTF commander supported by a component staff and MAGTF staff.

One-Commander/One-Staff Method

For smaller scaled operations, a one-commander and one-staff organization is used at the subordinate joint command level. This organization method is primarily used with a JTF but can be used for a subordinate unified command. In this method, the MAGTF commander and staff are also designated as the component commander and staff. The combatant command-level MARFOR can augment the component/MAGTF commander with personnel to establish an embedded component staff. Located with the MAGTF staff, the embedded staff concentrates on operational-level functions while the MAGTF staff focuses on tactical considerations.

Table 3-1. Levels of Marine Corps Componency and Organization.

Joint Force	Marine Corps Component	Organization
Combatant command	Combat command-level MARFOR	One commander and two staffs or two commanders and two staffs
Subordinate unified command or JTF	Subordinate joint command-level MARFOR	One commander and one staff

Command Responsibilities

C2 responsibilities for logistics are as follows:

● Joint staff and Services concentrate on strategic logistics.

● Supporting and supported combatant commander's logistic staff manage strategic and operational logistic issues that affect missions assigned to the combatant commanders in the Joint Strategic Capabilities Plan and other areas directed by the CINC.

● COMMARFOR or the senior MAGTF commander performs operational logistics. The COMMARFOR may establish a theater MLC to C2 operational-level logistic functions.

● MAGTF and subordinate commanders deal with tactical logistic responsibilities.

Marine Corps Forces Logistic Responsibilities

The focal point of Marine Corps operational logistic C2 is the MARFOR. The Marine Corps component is positioned at the confluence of the joint operational and Service administrative chains of command, the center of the theater distribution network, and the junction of the strategic/tactical logistic pipeline. Figure 3-2 depicts the central location of the Marine Corps component in the operational logistic C2 network. The MARFOR is responsible to the JFC for the following major actions:

● Making recommendations on the proper employment of MARFOR.

● Accomplishing operational missions assigned by the combatant commander.

● Selecting and nominating specific Marine units or forces for assignment to other subordinate forces of the combatant command.

● Conducting joint training and exercises.

● Informing the combatant commander of changes in planning for logistic support that will affect the combatant commander's ability to accomplish the mission.

● Developing Marine Corps programming and budgeting requests to support the combatant commander's warfighting requirements and priorities.

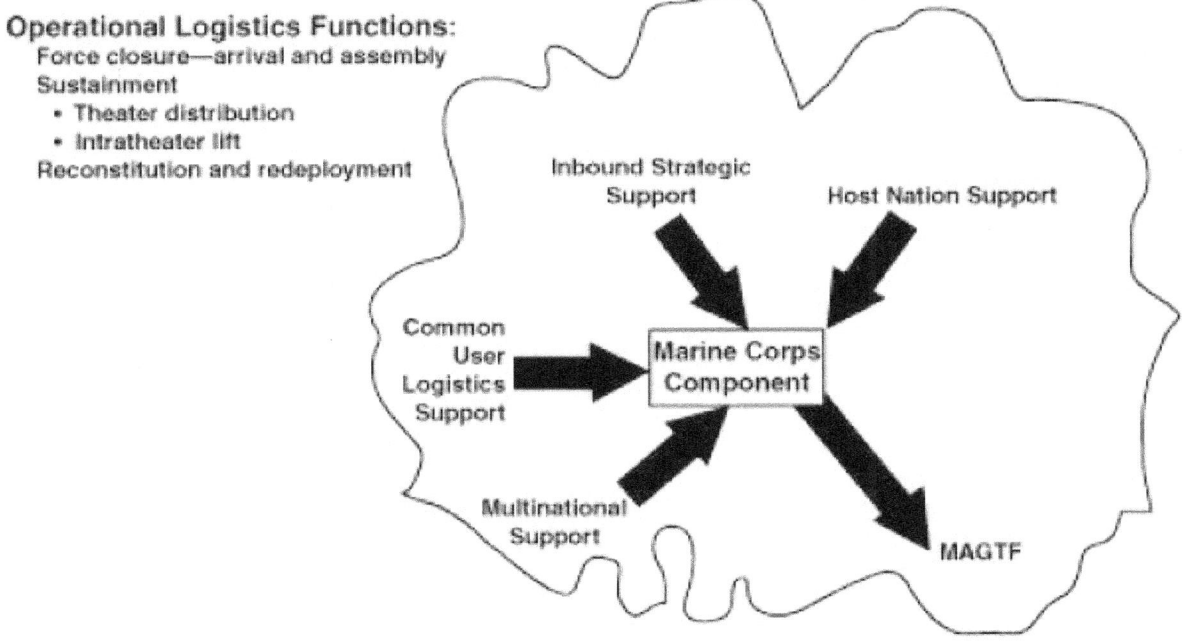

Figure 3-2. Operational Logistics C2.

- Providing supporting operation and exercise plans to support assigned missions.

Marine Corps Forces Command and Control Principles

To maximize the benefits from its central position, the MARFOR must interface effectively with joint and multinational organizations that use different processes than the Marine Corps. Multinational operations are difficult because of variations in language, terminology, doctrine, systems, and operating standards. To reduce confusion during joint and multinational theater logistic operations, the MARFOR is guided by the following C2 principles:

- Establish liaison early.
- Monitor current and evolving theater and Marine component logistic capabilities.
- Coordinate logistic support requirements with upcoming operations (in the construct of future operations and future plans).
- Advise the component commander on the supportability of proposed COAs.
- Coordinate with nontheater logistic organizations.
- Articulate Marine Corps capabilities and requirements to joint logistic centers, boards, and offices to coordinate the MARFOR logistic concept.
- Leverage limited C2 assets.
- Use U.S. interpreters.

- Use common cryptographic systems.
- Agree on policy in advance of war.

Marine Corps Forces Logistic Relationships

The MARFOR is responsible for planning, coordinating, and supervising the execution of operational logistic functions in support of the MAGTF as well as assigned and attached multinational and/or other Service forces. See figure 3-3.

Relationships with the Joint Force Commander

The JFC conducts the campaign by assigning subordinate commanders missions that accomplish strategic and operational objectives. The combatant commander exercises COCOM over the combatant command-level MARFOR, and the subordinate JFC exercises OPCON over a subordinate MARFOR.

Although the Service component is responsible for Service logistics, the JFC establishes operational logistic objectives and priorities. The JFC can designate a Service component to provide CUL to the joint force and/or establish a joint organization. Joint policy normally assigns CUL missions to a dominant user or most capable service.

Relationships between Marine Corps Forces

Marine Corps componency policy links MARFORs with each other, HQMC, and the Marine Corps SE. A subordinate MARFOR receives administrative

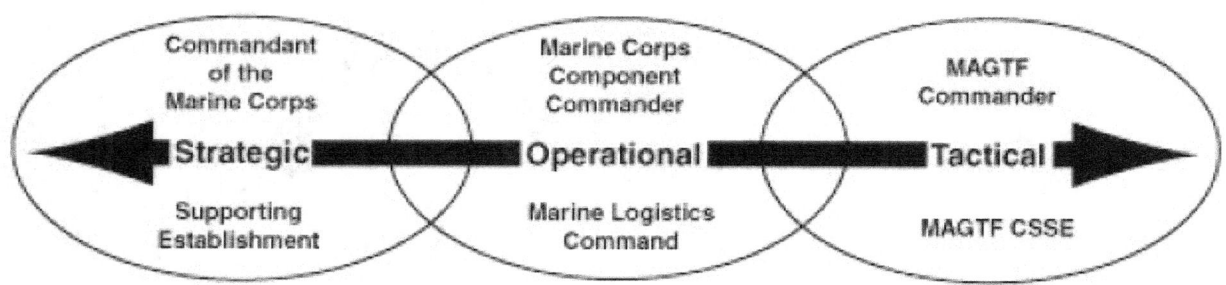

Figure 3-3. Level of War Orientation.

and logistic support from its parent combatant command-level MARFOR. For Service-specific matters, the subordinate MARFOR communicates directly with its parent MARFOR. When forces are attached from one combatant command-level MARFOR to another, the MARFOR providing the force and the MARFOR gaining the force should agree on and specify the support relationship for the attached forces. The Marine Corps SE and HQMC are responsible for providing the MARFOR logistics and administrative support.

The JFC may attach multinational and/or other Service forces to the MARFOR. Normally, logistics is a Service and national responsibility; however, the implementation of CUL arrangements may require the MARFOR to include and support the operational logistic requirements of non-Marine Corps units. The MARFOR remains responsible for informing the JFC on logistic issues affecting the execution of its mission.

Assistant Chief of Staff, G-4

The assistant chief of staff (AC/S), G-4, is the COMMARFOR's principal advisor for logistics. The focus of the MARFOR AC/S, G-4, is on planning, logistic policy, and coordination with agencies/Services external to the MAGTF for theater logistics.

The MARFOR G-4 is responsible for the following functions:

● Assisting the COMMARFOR in the development and implementation of logistic policy.
● Establishing priorities for the provision of logistics and allocation of logistic resources.
● Establishing the division of labor between the MLC, if established, and MAGTF.
● Setting the boundaries for direct liaison authorized (DIRLAUTH) for MARFOR logistic elements with external agencies.
● Coordinating nonaviation-peculiar logistics for MARFOR and other attached forces.
● Initiating and maintaining active liaison with HHQ, other Services, and allied forces.

● Designating the MLC or other MARFOR subordinate logistic agency as the liaison to selected joint boards and offices.

Supporting Marine Corps Forces

Depending on the circumstances, combatant command-level MARFORs can be either supporting or supported MARFORs. However, COMMARFORLANT and COMMARFORPAC are the established Marine Corps links to the Marine Corps operating forces, the Selected Marine Corps Reserve (SMCR), and most bases and stations in the SE.

From the operating forces, COMMARFORLANT and COMMARFORPAC can source logistic requirements from the peacetime operating stocks, remain-behind equipment (RBE), and war reserve materiel stocks field (WRMSF) under their control. Peacetime operating stocks are the everyday Marine Corps operating supplies (e.g., major end items and secondary items of equipment authorized by tables of equipment [T/Es]). RBE is the equipment that is left behind when an MPF MAGTF deploys or a MAGTF deploys that will use the geoprepositioned equipment and supplies in Norway. WRMSF is the portion of the war reserve materiel requirement held by the operating forces.

Relationships with Navy Aviation Commands

Commander, Naval Air Force, Pacific, and Commander, Naval Air Force, Atlantic, deal directly with the MAGTF ACE on aviation logistic matters. The Commander, Naval Air Force, Pacific, and Commander, Naval Air Force, Atlantic, are the aviation type commands within the Navy's chain of command. Although the ACE and the Navy-type commands have direct communications, the MAGTF commander must ensure that the MARFOR is fully knowledgeable on logistic matters affecting Marine Corp aviation. This information is required for the MARFOR to execute the responsibility of informing the JFC of any changes in logistic support that will affect the JFC's ability to accomplish the mission.

Relationships with Other Joint Force Component Commands

Joint policy encourages the Service components to coordinate, consult, and agree on common procedures and efficient use of logistic resources. The JFC may exercise DAL and establish joint support relationships. The JFC may direct the MARFOR to provide logistics to other Service units and personnel arriving early in theater. In addition, the JFC may use Marine Corps throughput organizations established during arrival and assembly operations as the nucleus for follow-on joint force closure. When the JFC directs a service component to provide CUL, the MARFOR coordinates with the supporting or supported components to ensure responsiveness of the support relationship directed.

Relationships with the MAGTF and Attached Forces

The MARFOR normally has OPCON and administrative control (ADCON) of the assigned and/or attached MAGTF. If the combatant commander attaches a MAGTF to a functional component, the MARFOR retains ADCON of the MAGTF. For attached forces from other Services and nations, the MARFOR normally coordinates with the providing Service component for the logistic support of attached forces. The JFC may define support relationships for attached forces in the operation or execute order.

While the MARFOR AC/S, G-4, focuses on planning, logistic policy, and external coordination for the theater campaign, the MLC executes COMMARFOR operational logistic responsibilities with an internal focus on supporting the MARFOR major subordinate commands. The external coordination by the MLC is with the MARFOR and joint logistic agencies responsible for the execution of theater logistics. The MARFOR will determine the best mix of external and organic Marine Corps sources to support the MAGTF. The MARFOR may task the MAGTF with providing the resources required for operational logistic functions. To the

extent possible, this should be determined during deliberate planning and during initial warning orders for crisis action planning to allow the MAGTF commander to properly task-organize forces.

Logistics Authority in Joint Operations

Unity of command requires responsibility and authority for logistics to support joint operations be vested in a single command authority. The single command authority improves effectiveness and efficiency while preventing unnecessary duplication of logistic effort among the Service components. The JFC exercises DAL through cross-servicing, common-servicing, and joint-servicing.

Joint Force Commander

To supervise and control logistic operations, the JFC may—

- Coordinate the total logistic effort through service components and other subordinate commands as required.
- Establish joint boards and offices as required to exercise control of logistics and promote economy of effort.
- Establish policies consistent with authority and existing JPs.
- Coordinate with other supporting commands to achieve long-term sustainment of forces.
- Prescribe and allocate common-user resources to components and subordinate commands.
- Use inter-Service support and common- or cross-servicing agreements to eliminate unnecessary duplication.
- Establish and coordinate priorities and programs to ensure effective use of supplies, facilities, and personnel.
- Review adequacy of service components' requirements consistent with service directives.
- Synchronize the concept of logistics with the concept of operations and ensure unity of effort.

Division Ready Brigade

During joint operations, an Army division ready brigade (DRB) may be attached to a MEF or a MEB. The DRB should come with its own forward support battalion (FSB) and a GS CSG(-) to augment FSSG. An FSB is similar in size and capability to an MSSG. The CSG(-) is task-organized based on the composition of the DRB and approximates a BSSG in size and capability. Figure 3-4 depicts the C2 logistics when the DRB operates under the control of the MEF.

Marine Expeditionary Brigade

With the exception of selected Class II, V (primarily aviation), VII, and IX supplies and mainte-

nance requirements peculiar to Marine Corps equipment, the Army can provide the majority of logistics required by the MEB that exceeds the capability of the CSSE. Figure 3-5 shows a notional corps support battalion (CSB) constituted to provide that support. CSB tailoring is contingent not only upon the support required by the MEB; its task organization would also accommodate support requirements for any additional Army elements placed under the control of or in support of the MEB. For example, the CSB would be task-organized with additional Class III and Class V capabilities to support a field artillery brigade placed in support of the MEB. Figure 3-6 on page 3-8 reflects the C2 relationship of logistic elements when the MEB operates as part of a corps.

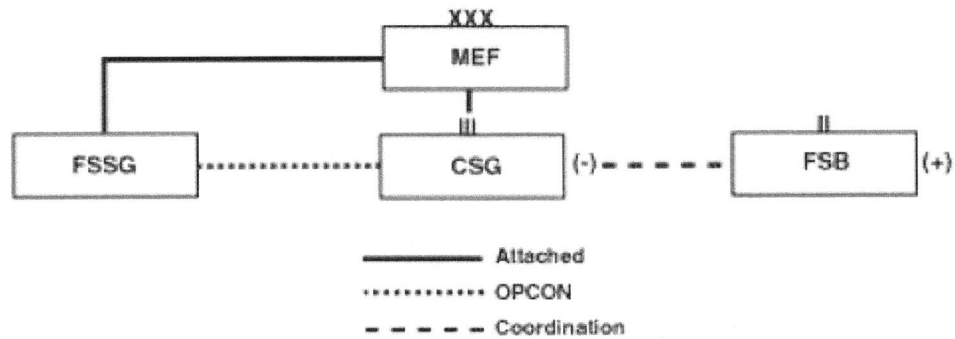

Figure 3-4. Logistics C2 DRB Under MEF Control.

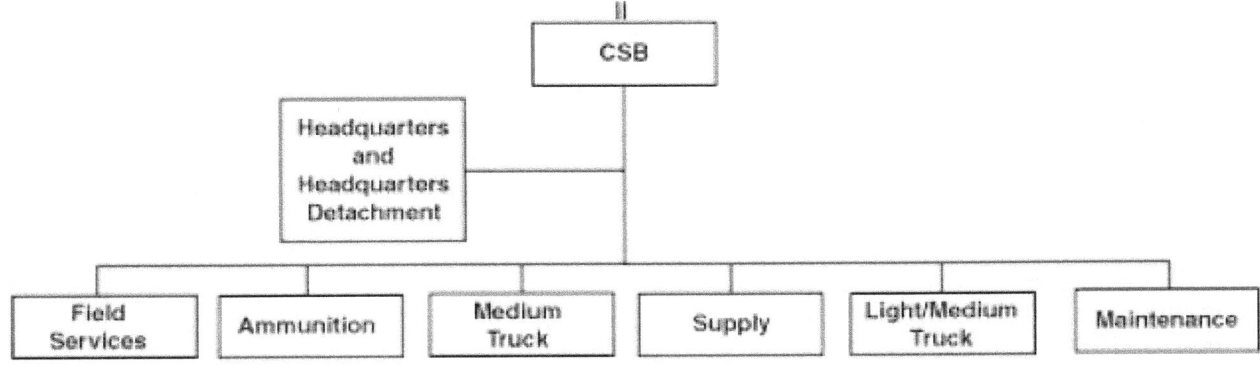

Figure 3-5. Notional CSB in Support of MEB.

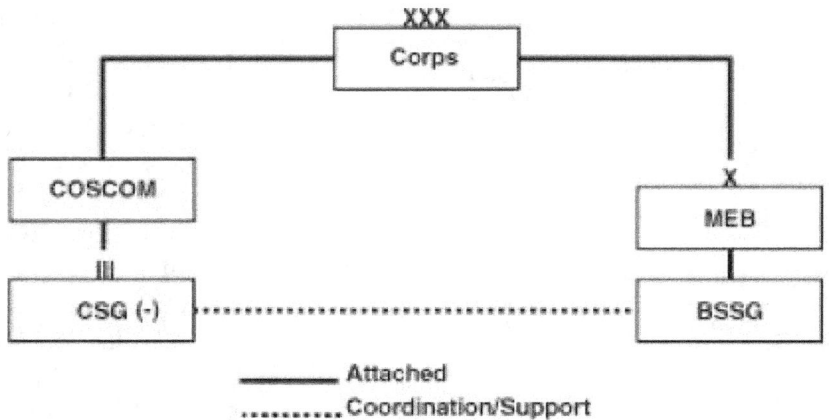

Figure 3-6. MEB Logistics C2 Under Corps Control.

Multinational Force Command and Control Relationships

National sovereignty restricts the command relationships available in an MNF. Ordinarily, forces from member nations have direct and near immediate communications to their respective national political leaderships. This link may facilitate coordination of issues, but it can also be a source of frustration as national leaders external to the operational area may be issuing guidance directly to their deployed national forces. Generally, the negative effects of direct national communications occur less in alliances, which are based on formal agreements and are of longer duration than coalitions. To establish a command structure, the MNFC must balance two, often-conflicting, conditions:

● Logistic economy and efficiency, through reduced redundancy and maximum use of CUL arrangements, best support combat operations.
● Individual nations are responsible for the logistic support of their forces.

Command Structures

Joint doctrine states that there is no single C2 structure or designation of authorities that best fits the needs of all alliances and coalitions. Accordingly, the structures established to C2 MNF operations must be adaptable to meet the needs of a particular operation. The MNFC can use the alliance integrated, lead nation, parallel, or a combination of parallel and lead nation command structures.

Alliance Integrated

In the alliance integrated command structure, the nationalities of the MNF headquarters staff and subordinate commands are different from the MNFC's nationality. See figure 3-7. Normally, the integrated command structure is used in an alliance situation of long duration (i.e., NATO). MNFs using this type of command structure have had the time to establish mutually agreed-on support systems and standardized procedures for C2 of logistic operations.

Lead Nation Command Structures

In a lead nation command structure, multinational members subordinate their forces to a single MNFC. See figure 3-8. The lead nation establishes logistic policies, procedures, and reporting requirements for the MNF In addition, the lead nation should ensure that participating national forces understand logistic requirements, which may require the preparation of packages that explain the lead nation's logistic policies, procedures, and reports. Used in alliance situations, the lead nation command structure is the preferred method for coalition operations.

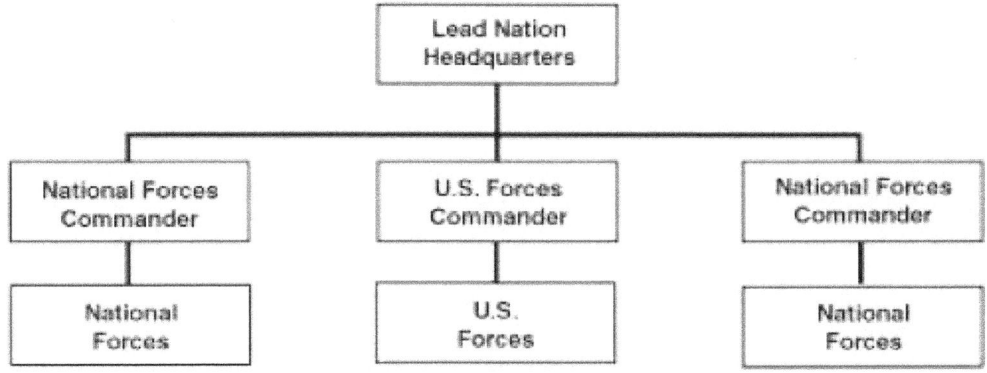

Figure 3-7. Alliance Integrated Command Structure.

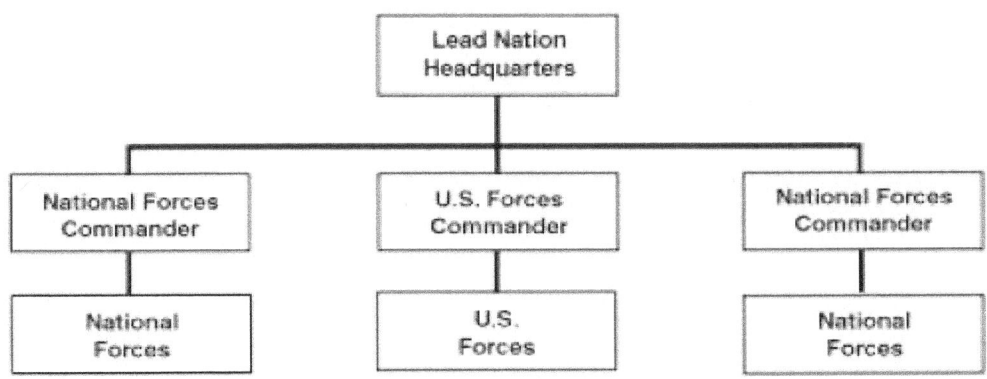

Figure 3-8. Lead Nation Command Structure.

Parallel Command Structure

In parallel command structure, separate but parallel national command structures exist to satisfy political/diplomatic requirements. National forces are not subordinate to a single commander. See figure 3-9 on page 3-10. CUL support is difficult. A centralized coordination center should be established between various command echelons to provide mutually beneficial logistics. Usually, the parallel command structure occurs in coalition operations.

Combination Parallel/Lead Nation Command Structure

In this structure, some multinational members have subordinated themselves to a single com-mander while other members have not. Effective C2 of logistics is extremely difficult to attain in such an arrangement. During Desert Storm, the U.S. led coalition used the parallel/lead nation command structure.

Command Relationships

The critical feature of multinational operations is that participants are from sovereign nations. Normally, this gives the MNFC minimum control over the different national forces in the command. For example, the CINC retains command authority over U.S. Forces attached to an MNF. This includes the authority and responsibility for using available

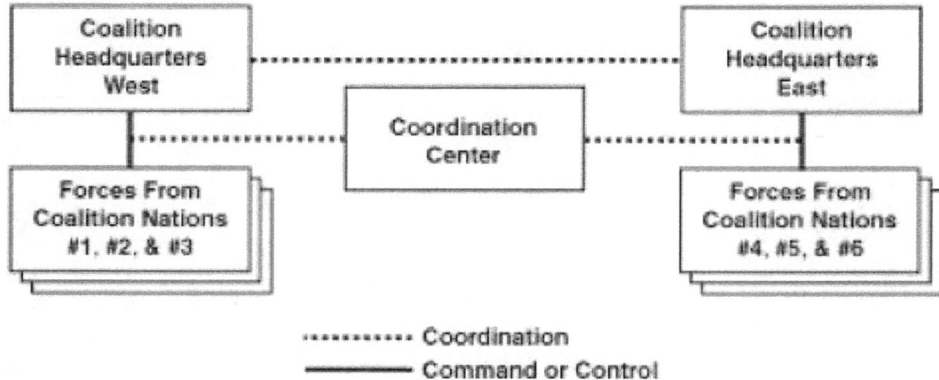

**Figure 3-9. Coalition Parallel Command Structure
(with Coordination Center).**

resources and for planning employment, organizing, directing, coordinating, controlling, and protecting the military force. The chain of command runs from the President to the lowest U.S. commander in the field and remains inviolate. U.S. commanders will maintain the capability to report separately to higher U.S. military authorities in addition to foreign commanders.

Other nations are as judicious in maintaining control over their own forces attached to an MNF. National authorities may allow another country to have OPCON, tactical control, and support relationships over their forces; however, coordinating authority will be the most probable command relationship used in multinational operations. Even when OPCON is granted to an MNFC, a nation will normally maintain a separate chain of command to their forces.

Coordination Centers

The use of coordination centers is an effective method for improving logistic C2 in a multinational operation. The coordination centers are valuable in facilitating unity of logistic effort in parallel C2 structures and can be established at the multinational joint and functional level. Functional coordination centers may be established to control logistic support operations, theater medical support, infrastructure engineering, and contracting. National forces should send staff members that are functionally proficient, speak a common language, and have adequate communications connectivity with their national commands.

Communications

The MARFOR headquarters is the hub of operational level of war activities and requires extensive communications connectivity. However, the requirement to support a deployable MARFOR headquarters with communications and information systems (CIS) personnel and equipment can have a significant effect on the availability of CIS resources to support the MAGTF.

Communications Battalion

The primary source of support to the MARFOR is the MEF's communications battalion. It installs, operates, and maintains communications for the MARFOR headquarters, MEF CE, and MEB CE. The MEF communications battalion is also responsible for message and voice switches and links to joint force headquarters, major subordinate commands, adjacent units, the naval telecommunications system, and the Defense Communications System. Joint doctrine states that the communications battalion may be augmented for joint operations by joint force-provided communications systems.

Marine Logistics Command

The MLC must be able to communicate internally within the component and externally with the host nation, joint agencies, multinational organizations, other component headquarters, and the strategic base. Internally, the MLC relies on the FSSG communications company for connectivity with subordinate commands and elements. The communications capability may be sourced from the supported FSSG depending on the tactical situation, Marine forces available, and the MARFOR logistic support concept. The communications company establishes connectivity between the MLC headquarters and subordinate CSSEs. Within the MARFOR, the supporting communications element establishes connectivity among the MLC, the MARFOR, and the supported FSSG. The MLC communicates with external organizations to the MARFOR through the circuits established for the MARFOR by the communications battalion.

Command, Control, Communications, and Computer Systems

Advancements in information technology and communications are improving command, control, communications, and computers (C4) capabilities. C4 systems developed for strategic or tactical use can be applied at the operational level. The Global Combat Support System (GCSS), Global Command and Control System (GCCS), and Joint Operation Planning and Execution System (JOPES) are logistic information management systems that improve the planning and execution of operational logistic functions.

Global Combat Support System

The GCSS provides integration and interoperability between combat support functions and C2 to support the operational needs of the warfighter. It directly supports command, control, communications, computers, and intelligence. Using the defense information infrastructure (DII) and/or common operating environment (COE) as well as the shared data environment, GCSS ensures rapid integration of combat support applications by providing a seamless flow of operational and sustaining base information to the warfighter. GCSS provides accurate and near real time total asset visibility vital to the deployment, employment, sustainment, reconstitution, and redeployment of joint combat assets or resources.

The GCSS portal is a web-based, online query capability to access fused and integrated combat support data. It consists of a set of applications that may be accessible individually or directly from the common operational picture (COP)-client server environment (CSE). Current combat support applications on the GCSS portal are accessible via a unilateral log-on feature through public key infrastructure technology.

Global Command and Control System

The GCCS is a graphical depiction of warfighting information available in an AOR. A key tool for commanders planning and conducting joint operations, GCCS enhances the flow of information between the NCA, joint staff, and commanders by amplifying situation reports (SITREPs), operational reports (OPREPs), and other key reports. GCCS displays battlespace information in a graphical manner that links to detailed information, which SITREPs and OPREPs are unable to display. The GCCS provides the user interface to access combat support and CSS applications such as Global

Transportation Network (GTN) and joint total asset visibility (JTAV). The GCCS provides direct combat support (e.g., logistic, transportation, medical, personnel) information to warfighters.

Global Transportation Network and Joint Total Asset Visibility

Among the joint automated systems that will enable GCSS are GTN and JTAV. The GTN is a global C2 information repository designed to track DOD unit and non-unit cargo and passengers while in transit. JTAV allows timely and accurate information on the location, movement, status, and identity of units, personnel, equipment, and supplies. JTAV integrates in-process, in-storage, or in-transit visibility (ITV). ITV refers to the ability to track the identity, status, and location of DOD unit and non-unit cargo, passengers, and medical patients from origin to the foxhole, during peace, contingencies, and war. GTN provides the ITV that is integrated with JTAV.

Joint Decision Support Tools

The joint decision support tools (JDSTs) provide warfighters and logisticians with the ability to access support force capabilities to perform mission tasks, develop and evaluate logistic operational support plans, monitor logistic operations, and react to deviations from project support. The JDSTs are available via a web-based, client-server environment that complies with DII and COE architecture standards and requirements.

Joint Operation Planning and Execution System

The JOPES is the integrated C2 system used to plan and execute joint military operations. JOPES includes joint operation planning policies, procedures, and reporting structures supported by communications and automated data processing on GCCS. Marine Corps planners use these applications for deployment and employment planning. The following systems feed MAGTF logistic requirements into JOPES.

MAGTF II/Logistic Automated Information System

The Marine air-ground task force system II (MAGTF II)/logistic automated information system (LOGAIS) supports Marine Corps ground logistic data requirements. Marine Corps planners use MAGTF II to create operations plans. The MAGTF II system is the primary planning tool for selecting and tailoring a MAGTF and for providing updates to JOPES. It includes Transportation Coordinator's Automated Information for Movement System (TC-AIMS) and the MAGTF Deployment Support System II (MDSS II).

Transportation Coordinator's Automated Information for Movement System. The TC-AIMS provides automated support for motor transport control, planning of support, and coordination of overland movement and convoys. Managing use and movement of day-to-day motor transport and heavy equipment, TC-AIMS resource-management module provides inventory, support requests, and task and dispatch management. In addition, TC-AIMS supports convoy management with an embarkation and marshaling module. This system also tracks critical events, including user-time statistics.

MAGTF Deployment Support System II. The MDSS II assists in deployment planning and execution and unit movement at the MEF level and below. It functions in coordination with TC-AIMS.

Asset Tracking Logistics and Supply System

The Asset Tracking Logistics and Supply System (ATLASS) provides automated support for supply and maintenance. It replaces the Marine Integrated Maintenance Management System (MIMMS) and the supported activities supply system (SASSY). ATLASS is being implemented through phased development, with the current phase focusing on integrating user unit supply and shop-level maintenance functions. ATLASS will provide functional logistic management for sustainment and distribution information to MAGTF II/LOGAIS.

Navy Support Systems

Three Navy systems support Marine Corps aviation.

Shipboard Nontactical Automated Data Processing Program III

The MALS uses Shipboard Nontactical Automated Data Processing Program III (SNAP III) hardware to provide automated information processing support for supply, finance, and organizational maintenance management.

Naval Aviation Logistics Command Management Information System

The MALS uses the Naval Aviation Logistics Command Management Information System (NALCOMIS) software application to provide automated information processing support for maintenance of aviation equipment and spares to aviation units and selected base and garrison activities throughout the Marine Corps.

Shipboard Uniform Automated Data Processing System

The Shipboard Uniform Automated Data Processing System (SUADPS) supply software application is used by the MALS to provide financial, inventory, and logistic management of aviation supply support for Marine aircraft.

CHAPTER 4. PLANNING

Planning is the act of envisioning a desired end state and determining effective ways of achieving that goal. It supports the commander in making decisions in a time-constrained and uncertain environment. To attain the desired end state, the joint community and the Marine Corps have developed highly structured, comprehensive, and compatible planning procedures. Operational logistic planners on the MARFOR, MEF, and FSSG staffs participate along with other functional specialists in determining the best plans to accomplish the mission. They must work closely with MAGTF and joint force planners to coordinate and synchronize mutually understood and supportable plans.

Objectives

The objective of operational-level logistic planning is to match the Marine Corps deployment and sustainment activities and joint logistic systems with the requirements of the MAGTF. Through participation in the planning process, logisticians gain situational awareness and compile ready, relevant, and realistic data to support deliberate or time-sensitive planning requirements. Detailed planning outlines the means of providing CSS to the MAGTF based on the conceptual and functional planning goals and objectives.

Conceptual

Conceptual planning establishes goals, objectives, and the broad schemes for achieving them. Participation in conceptual planning enables the operational-level logistic planner to ensure operational concepts are supportable and shapes the requirements for preparing functional and detailed plans. Conceptual planners must—

- Integrate logistic requirements with existing plans and annexes.

- Determine basic, broad mobilization, deployment, and sustainment requirements.
- Determine theater organization and conduct logistic preparation of the theater.
- Consider battlespace geometry, real estate requirements, movement control, and their impact on logistic bottlenecks.
- Determine critical and vital supplies.
- Allocate resources.

Functional

Functional planning designs supporting plans for discrete logistic activities such as deployment plans, marshalling and movement plans, sustainment plans, and concepts of logistics and CSS. Marine Corps functional planning usually encompasses force deployment planning and sustainment planning, which are two logistics-related planning areas critical to the development and maintenance of combat power. Maintaining a single battle approach, functional planners focus on logistics to—

- Provide instructions or guidance for redistributing assets from low- to high-priority organizations within the command.
- Source known requirements and anticipate unidentified requirements.
- Determine size and location of logistic facilities and units.
- Provide efficient means to retrograde, repair, and redistribute critical items.

Tasks

Coordinating and managing operational-level logistic functions involves support activities required to sustain campaigns and major operations. Theater logistic organizations provide resources by identifying or developing intermediate and forward support bases, establishing an effective transportation system, coordinating with joint operational logistic infrastructure in theater, and supporting force closure. The MARFOR is responsible for coordinating and supervising the following planning tasks:

- Identifying force logistic requirements.
- Coordinating and supervising force closure and onward movement.
- Organizing MARFOR logistic support through the COMMZ.
- Developing agreements with other component commands and participating in component command-level working groups.
- Continuously refining force personnel, sustainment, transportation, and reception requirements.
- Informing the JFC of changes in logistic requirements that might affect Marine Corps operations.
- Sourcing MARFOR requirements from the Marine Corps, other Service components, joint, HNS, or multinational agencies.
- Allocating intratheater transportation assets.
- Developing theater facilities.
- Implementing ACSAs to fill MAGTF requirements and coordinate HNS.
- Coordinating MARFOR contingency contracting with the JFC chief of contracting.
- Coordinating and integrating HSS in the theater of war with the JFS or senior medical regulating authority.
- Coordinating and supervising reconstitution and redeployment.
- Ensuring the effectiveness and economy of Marine Corps operational-level logistics.
- Developing and coordinating a plan for RBE.

Processes

Operational-level logistic planners participate in the Marine Corps Planning Process (MCPP) and use JOPES for deliberate and crisis action planning. The MCPP is an internal planning process used by the Marine Corps operating forces. Marine Corps Warfighting Publication (MCWP) 5-1,

Marine Corps Planning Process, describes the MCPP, which is aligned with and complements, the joint planning processes found in JP 5-0, *Doctrine for Planning Joint Operations.* When designated as a JFC or preparing a supporting plan to a campaign, a commander and staff use JOPES and the MCPP. Plans, orders, and reports should adhere to JOPES formats.

Joint Operation Planning and Execution System

Joint operation planning encompasses planning activities required for conducting joint operations. These activities include the mobilization, deployment, employment, sustainment, and redeployment of forces. Conducted under JOPES policy, procedures, and automated data processing support, joint operational planning is a coordinated process used by a commander to determine the best method of accomplishing the mission. In peacetime, the process is called deliberate planning. In crises, it is called crisis action planning.

There are three types of planning at the joint level: deliberate planning, crisis action planning, and campaign planning. Deliberate and crisis action planning have distinct processes. Campaign planning uses the deliberate and crisis action processes for developing plans.

The TPFDD is the database portion of an OPLAN contained in JOPES. It contains time-phased force data, nonunit-related cargo and personnel data, and movement data for the OPLAN. The TPFDD contains the following information:

- In-place units.
- Deploying units to support the OPLAN with a priority indicating the sequence for their arrival at the port of debarkation.
- Routes of deploying forces.
- Movement data of deploying forces.
- Estimates of nonunit-related cargo and personnel movements to be conducted concurrently with the deployment of forces.

• Estimate of transportation requirements that must be fulfilled by common-user lift resources and those requirements that can be fulfilled by assigned or attached transportation resources.

Force Deployment Planning and Execution

Marine Corps planning and execution have been described as force deployment planning and execution (FDP&E). FDP&E supports the maneuver of forces and their sustainment within a battlespace based on the concept of employment. A total operational effort, FDP&E includes the planning and execution of logistic tasks to support mission accomplishment. See Marine Corps Order (MCO) P3000.18, *Marine Corps Planners Manual*, for a detailed description of FDP&E.

Principal Planning Agencies

Operational-level logistic planning is in the realm of the combatant command-level COMMARFOR and logistic staff, and the MAGTF commander and logistic staff. The combatant command-level MARFOR and MEF are higher-level commands that have specialized planning staff elements and organizations to conduct planning. Lower-level commands consist of subordinate MARFORs, MEB, SPMAGTF, ACM, MEU, and their CSSEs. At the lower level, the unit's commander and primary staff officers conduct most planning. Because resources, information, and time available for planning are usually limited at the lower command levels, planning organizations are formed or adapted to meet conditions.

Higher-level commands have a specialized planning staff to conduct current and future operations planning. Operational-level logistic planners participate in the organization's activities and teams that conduct planning at the Marine component command and MAGTF level. Figure 4-1 on page 4-4 illustrates the planning

organizations and relations of the MARFOR, MLC, MEF, and the joint force.

Plans Section

This section plans the command's next mission, next phase of the campaign, or peacetime deliberate planning and serves as the link between HHQ and future operations. Upon receipt of a mission from HHQ, future plans initiates planning and develops an outline plan. Plans section may focus on a phase of a campaign, develop reconstitution requirements, or plan redeployment. Normally, the G-5 has staff cognizance over the plans section.

Future Operations Section

Future operations is the focal point for the planning process. It takes the outline plan from the plans section and uses it as the basis for further planning and development of orders and fragmentary orders. Depending on the level of command and HHQ battle rhythms, future operations have a 24- to 96-hour planning horizon. The G-3 has staff cognizance over the future operations section, which interacts with the intelligence collection process.

Future operations section creates OPORDs and branch and sequel plans. It assists the commander in developing commander's critical information requirements (CCIR), which express the commander's critical needs for information about the enemy, friendly activities, and the environment. In addition, future operations section provides input to HHQ PDE&A cycles (e.g., air tasking order, intelligence asset tasking cycle).

Operational Planning Team

Plans and/or operations may form an operational planning team (OPT) to conduct integrated planning. The OPT is normally built around a core of planners from future plans and/or future operations and includes staff representatives from the

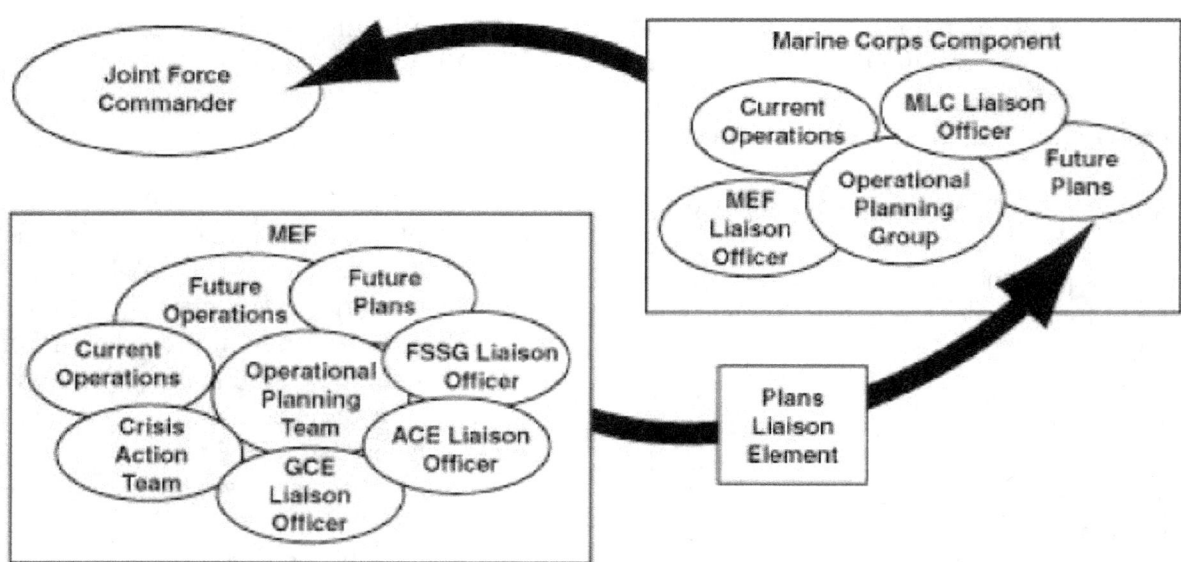

Figure 4-1. Component and MEF Planning Agencies.

G-1, G-2, G-3 G-4, G-5, G-6, staff judge advocate, health services, public affairs, etc. The FSSG will normally provide an LNO to participate in MEF OPTs.

Current Operations Section

The current operations section coordinates and executes the OPORD, prepares and transmits tactical orders, monitors operations, tracks CCIR, reports relevant information to the commander, and analyzes battlespace information. Based on the situation, current operations, commander's intent, and battle feedback, this section modifies orders, refines branch plans, generates new COAs and/or plans, and issues tactical orders. The G-3 has staff cognizance over the current operations section.

Crisis Action Team

During the initial stages of a crisis, the G-3 usually task-organizes the crisis action team (CAT) to rapidly collect and manage information. To support the commander's primary concern for force readiness and deployment planning in the initial stage of a crisis, the CAT may initiate the planning process, develop situational awareness,

and access previously prepared and emerging planning products from JOPES. For extended operations, the planning and execution functions of the CAT will transition to the current operations, future operations, and plans sections.

Concept of Logistics

The concept of logistics is a statement, in a broad outline, of how a commander intends to support and integrate with the concept of operations during an operation or campaign. The statement provides a general discussion of how the operation will be logistically supported and integrated with other critical concepts (e.g., the concept of maneuver, fires, and force protection). It should be composed with enough depth to ensure that subordinate commanders and staffs understand the envisioned logistic operations. The concept of logistics should describe the organization and positioning of operational logistic assets to execute the mission. The concept may include planned employment of other Service and nation logistic/CSS forces, HNS logistic capabilities, and/or LOC operations.

The concept of logistics is developed concurrently with the concept of operations. The concept of operations is a description of the operation and includes a statement of a commander's intent for an operation or series of operations and is the basis for supporting concepts such as the concept of logistics. The concepts of operations and logistics evolve from the early steps of the planning process, which culminates in the commander's selection of a COA. The selected COA serves as the basis for the commander's estimate, while the analysis of that COA formulated in the logistic estimate serves as the basis for the concept of logistics.

Intelligence

Providing knowledge on the theater environment and potential enemy activities, intelligence builds situational awareness and insight into the nature of operational logistic limitations and challenges facing MARFOR commanders. Commanders use intelligence products to devise workable, flexible plans; make sound and timely decisions; monitor events to ensure proper execution; and modify decisions quickly in response to changing situations or to exploit fleeting opportunities. A detailed list of possible logistic intelligence requirements (IRs) can be found in the *Generic Intelligence Requirements Handbook (GIRH)* available through the Marine Corps Intelligence Agency and other intelligence agencies.

Logistic IRs focus on the study of roads, rails, bridges, tunnels, fords, choke points, ports, airfields, and infrastructure and how they tie together in support of logistic operations. A majority of logistic intelligence studies are prepared using open-source historical and encyclopedic data. A logistic infrastructure study helps identify—

- Water sources.
- Local communications systems.
- Local transportation systems.

- Bridges.
- Tunnel restrictions.
- Waterway capabilities.
- Road networks.
- Local sources of supply.
- Power production facilities.
- Medical assistance programs.
- Food distribution networks.
- Capability for care of displaced persons.

Environment

Knowledge of the theater environment, to include infrastructure, weather and terrain, medical, and host-nation populace intelligence, is a critical requirement for operational logistic planners. The quality of the theater's resource and physical networks affect the size and composition of the MAGTF's CSSE and the MLC, the amount of resources required from the strategic base, and the level of effort needed to establish a theater distribution network.

Infrastructure

Infrastructure intelligence is information on existing infrastructure, such as ports, factories, fuel, water sources, LOC, medical facilities, and other in-country resources that can be used to support logistic operations.

Weather and Terrain

Weather and terrain affect resource consumption and logistic operations. Weather information addresses the weather conditions prevailing, or predicted to prevail, over the theater of operations. Terrain analysis consists of the collection, evaluation, and interpretation of geographic information on the natural and manmade features of the terrain, combined with other relevant factors, to predict the effect of the terrain on military operations.

Medical

Medical intelligence is required to ascertain theater medical capabilities and the medical threat to the MARFOR. The intelligence from the collection, evaluation, analysis, and interpretation of foreign medical, bio-scientific, and environmental information is of interest to strategic planning and to military medical planning and operations for the conservation of the fighting strength of friendly forces and the formation of assessments of foreign medical capabilities in both military and civilian sectors.

Host Nation Populace

Intelligence about the populace, their capabilities, and attitude toward U.S. Forces has a significant impact on logistics. A receptive, friendly populace may be able to provide dependable labor, supplies, and contract services.

This can reduce footprint and enhance flexibility, responsiveness, and economy of logistics. A hostile environment not only dictates organic provision of supplies and logistic services, but it also increases the threat in rear areas and along LOC.

Threat

An accurate picture of the enemy is critical to logistic operations. Analysis of the threat can also help logisticians anticipate requirements (e.g., mobility infrastructure repair capabilities, medical threats from specific types of munitions). Hostile activities can impede movement, destroy logistic stockpiles, and close airports and seaports. Hostile actions can render invalid logistic support assumptions made during deliberate planning. Threat information should include enemy logistic capabilities.

Logistic planners use the threat information to recommend enemy stockpiles and equipment for capture or destruction. The intelligence threat assessment also identifies threat shortfalls so

appropriate steps can be taken to safeguard friendly like items against capture or sabotage.

Collection Support

Certain intelligence activities—such as interrogation of EPW and the recovery and evacuation of enemy equipment—require logistic support and/or coordination with MARFOR and MLC logistic planners. The Marine Corps component is the theater focal point for planning and the source for operational-level logistic intelligence. Through representation and coordination with theater intelligence boards, agencies, and headquarters, the Marine component expresses IRs and ensures that intelligence products are directly provided to the MAGTF, the MLC, and other assigned or attached forces. The Marine Corps component coordinates intelligence collection requirements, such as EPW interrogation and captured enemy equipment (CEE), to support the joint force collection plan.

Enemy Prisoner of War

Normally, the Army component commander, or MARFOR, will be designated to establish an EPW compound that will include facilities and logistics for a collocated joint interrogation and debriefing center (JIDC). To establish a JIDC with an EPW compound, MARFOR logistic and intelligence planners must coordinate their efforts.

Captured Enemy Equipment

The recovery and evacuation of CEE is a command responsibility. The proper handling of CEE requires close coordination among operations, logistic, and intelligence departments. Enemy materiel captured by U.S. military personnel is the property of the U.S. Government and must be protected from theft, cannibalization, use as souvenirs or war trophies, and recapture by enemy forces. The MARFOR coordinates CEE handling and recovery procedures with the joint force.

Sources

During the planning process, Marine Corps component, MLC, and FSSG planners can request or obtain operational-level logistic intelligence by using intelligence preparation of the battlespace (IPB), intelligence production organizations, and organic unit human intelligence sources.

Intelligence Preparation of the Battlespace

IPB is an analytical methodology employed to reduce operational uncertainties concerning the enemy, environment, and terrain. IPB builds an extensive database for each potential area where a unit may be required to operate. The database is analyzed in detail to determine the impact of the enemy, environment, and terrain on operations. Planners use HHQ's IPB products during mission analysis and update the IPB during the planning process.

Production Organizations

The following intelligence production organizations provide logistic intelligence on seaports, airfields, threat, noncombatants, and infrastructure:

- Defense Intelligence Agency (DIA).
- Operational Intelligence Coordination Center.
- USTRANSCOM.
- Marine Corps Intelligence Agency.
- National Imagery and Mapping Agency.
- Central Intelligence Agency.

Organic Unit Human Intelligence

During operations, tactical organizations such as CSSEs can be an excellent source of intelligence updates. Convoys, mobile CSSEs, and individual drivers (military and local contracted) travel throughout the AO on a daily basis. These units can provide updated information on the location and status of roads, trails, and waterways to update map products. MARFOR and FSSG logistic planners should establish feedback plans to take advantage of this source of intelligence updates.

Host-Nation Support

HNS is the civil and/or military assistance rendered by a nation to foreign forces within its territory during peacetime, crises, emergencies, or war based on agreements mutually concluded between nations. The development of HNS agreements is usually based on a status-of-forces agreement between the host nation and the United States. Such agreements are normally umbrella-type agreements, augmented by technical arrangements that detail the specific support to be provided and the type/amount of reimbursement. In some cases, reimbursement may not be required because the host nation recognizes the importance of foreign forces on their territory and considers their HNS to be a contribution to the security arrangement. Each country or region is unique in its approach to HNS. In the absence of a formal support arrangement, the MAGTF can contract local supplies and services in the AO.

HNS agreements are usually established in diplomatic channels, however, during crises, the geographic combatant commander may request authority to negotiate bilateral agreements.

Logistic planners identify, evaluate, and determine host-nation sources of supplies and services to be used during the operation. Information on existing agreements can be obtained from existing OPLANs and from requests to HHQ for information formulated during the mission analysis phase of planning. Information regarding HNS can also be obtained from legal and civil affairs units, the DIA, the appropriate area LNO at the Defense Security Cooperation Agency, and from contact with local authorities in the host nation. The types of support that can be obtained and/or contracted from a host nation include—

- Transportation.
- Civilian labor.
- Rear area protection.
- Acquisition of equipment.
- Airlift services.

- Port services.
- Clothing.
- Base operations support.
- Calibration services.
- HSS.
- Facilities.
- Petroleum, oils, and lubricants (POL).
- Food.
- Communications.
- Storage services.
- Billeting.
- Maintenance services.
- Construction equipment.

Contingency Contracting

U.S. Forces have the ability to contract goods and services directly from the local economy. In arranging support for the MAGTF, the MARFOR may use contingency contracting to obtain goods and services. The level of support differs from country to country and must be thoroughly analyzed by the MARFOR during the planning process and constantly reassessed during employment. The MARFOR must weigh the impact of contingency contracting on the local economy.

Contracting may compete for scarce resources, strain the local economy, and exacerbate an already unstable situation. The CINC or combined headquarters may establish a centralized contingency contracting office that coordinates contracting activities. Joint contracting helps to keep prices down, minimize negative impact on the local economy, and settle conflicts between Services.

Contingency contracting is performed during military operations in an overseas location following the policies and procedures of the Federal Acquisition Regulatory System. Marine Corps contractors may acquire supplies and services from theater resources such as NGOs, foreign governments, and individual civilian providers. Planning should address theater sources and the early deployment of contingency contractors to a theater of war. Contracting in the operations area must be coordinated with the overall operations concept to ensure logistic measures do not compromise other facets of the operations. Enemy forces can use contracting to gather information of U.S. Forces' strength, movement plans, arrival timelines, and billeting locations.

Logistic shortfalls will likely occur early in the deployment of a force. To offset this possibility, a contingency contracting capability should be established as soon as possible. Contracting officers assigned to an expeditionary operation should have a basic understanding of the legal authorities, funding practices, and the duties of contingency contracting.

Unlike HNS, in-country sources do not have formal agreements between nations that planners can easily obtain and analyze as potential sources of support. Information on local sources is harder to determine but can be obtained from the same sources as HNS.

The following considerations influence planning for the early deployment of contracting personnel:

- Protection of contractor personnel.
- Assignment of an in-theater head of contracting activity for U.S. Forces participating in the operation.
- Use of third country subcontractors and/or personnel.
- Limitations on the physical presence of contractors (i.e., boundaries within which contractors are to operate).
- Payment of customs duties by contractors when entering the country.
- Payment of corporate and/or individual taxes.
- Payment by contractors of taxes on goods bought within the country/AO.

Environmental matters such as transportation and disposal criteria and locations for hazardous waste and scrap.

Acquisition Cross-Service Agreements

ACSAs are bilateral agreements used for the mutual exchange of supplies and services. The purpose of ACSA is to further the CINC's strategy of cooperative engagement by promoting interoperability, enhancing operational readiness, and providing cost effective mutual support.

Types of Authority

The proposed ACSA with a given country must be in the interest of U.S. National security per consultation between the Secretary of Defense (SECDEF) and the Secretary of State. Two types of authorities within ACSA are acquisitions and cross-service agreements.

Acquisition

Unified combatant commands determine eligibility for acquisitions. SECDEF can authorize acquisition of supplies and services from those countries that—

- Have a defense alliance with the United States.
- Permit stationing of U.S. Forces or home porting of U.S. naval vessels.
- Allow pre-positioning of U.S. materials.
- Host exercise or other military operations (U.S. Military Forces acquiring supplies and services directly from eligible countries and organizations do not require an ACSA).

Cross-Servicing Agreements

Applicable supplies and services are acquired or transferred by the United States on the basis of reimbursement, replacement in kind (RIK), or

exchange of supplies or services of an equal value. For non-NATO countries to participate in this program, SECDEF must designate the country. This requires an ACSA agreement. The SECDEF submits notice of the intended designation to congressional committees 30 days in advance.

After SECDEF designation, unified combatant commands negotiate cross-service agreements. Services or components negotiate implementing arrangements with counterparts. An implementing arrangement provides the mechanics and points of contact to make the ACSA work. Accounting, reporting, billing, and collecting are Service responsibilities.

Supplies and Services

The ACSA covers supplies, services, and support, including airlift. Repayment is by reimbursement, RIK, or equal value exchange. Components can use the ACSA for obtaining the following supplies and services:

- Food.
- Transportation, including airlift and helicopter support.
- Clothing.
- Medical services.
- Base operations support.
- Facilities usage.
- Spare parts/components.
- Port services.
- Billeting.
- POL.
- Communications services.
- Ammunition.
- Storage services.
- Training services.
- Repairs and maintenance.

Planning Documents

Several planning documents in the MCPP and joint planning process are essential for logistic planning. Instructions and formats for command and staff estimates, OPLANS, OPORDS, and annexes, and appendixes are contained in MCWP 5-1 and Chairman Joint Chief of Staff Manual (CJCSM) 3122.03, *Joint Operation Planning and Execution System Volume II Planning Format and Guidance*.

CHAPTER 5. OPERATIONS

To support operations, the Marine Corps developed extensive operational-level logistic capabilities, as a single Service and in cooperation with the Navy. Other Services have vast capabilities and may provide single-Service logistics to MARFOR. In addition to providing operational logistics to the MAGTF during expeditionary operations, the MARFOR may be tasked by the JFC to provide CUL to the joint force, especially during the early phases of joint force deployment and initial entry operations. As the MEF's major subordinate command capable of operating at tactical and operational levels of war, the FSSG provides operational-level logistics in the Marine Corps by employing functionally structured battalions.

Force Service Support Group Employment

The functional battalion structure of the FSSG provides a common point of departure for the many possible task-organized CSSEs employed for operations or as the basis for an operational logistic organization (i.e., MLC). The FSSG employs various sized CSSEs vice the functional battalion organization based on METT-T and force size.

The FSSG employs CSSDs in a DS role to GCE maneuver elements and ACE units. Mobile combat service support detachments (MCSSDs) are employed in support of mechanized/armor maneuver elements. Larger GS CSSGs or CSSDs are employed to support several units within the MAGTF that do not have DS CSSDs. In addition, a GS CSSG or CSSD may provide a reinforcing role to several DS CSSDs. The FSSG may maintain some battalions in a GS role, such as maintenance battalion (-) or supply battalion (-) to operate the intermediate maintenance activity or intermediate supply activity. Other battalions may be reinforced and redesignated CSSG/CSSD. Figure 5-1 on page 5-2 shows the 1st FSSG task organization

for Operation Desert Storm and provides examples of CSSE employment.

MARFOR and FSSG logistic planners must develop sequels to plans that anticipate the growth of the CSSE task-organization as the theater develops. Planners should consider the role of the functional battalions as they are drawn down to support task-organized units. Redesignation, renumbering, and reorganization of CSSEs should be minimized. Excessive reorganization can complicate equipment readiness reporting, personnel accountability, and casualty reporting. Finally, planners should consider the role of regiment/group-level CSSEs as an FSSG is reinforced.

A CSSG is a task organization of CSS assets, similar in size and capability to a BSSG. A CSSG is formed to provide CSS to a large GCE task force, reinforce regiment, or composite MAG conducting independent operations or geographically separated from the MEF. A CSSG is capable of task-organizing subordinate CSSDs. Currently, 1st FSSG has CSSG-1 established to support 7th Marines (Rein) at Twentynine Palms, CA, and 3d FSSG has CSSG-3 established to support 3d Marines (Rein) and the aviation support element at Kaneohe Bay, HI.

Marine Logistics Command Operations

The MLC is an organizational and command option that the COMMARFOR may choose to employ. The MLC MTW concept emerged from Operations Desert Shield and Desert Storm. During that MTW, 1st FSSG provided GS to I MEF from the COMMZ through General Support Group 1 (GSG-1). The commanding generals of the merged FSSGs coordinated to switch logistic units between the two commands. Thus, the optimal combination of logistic assets supported the operational-level logistic functions and tactical

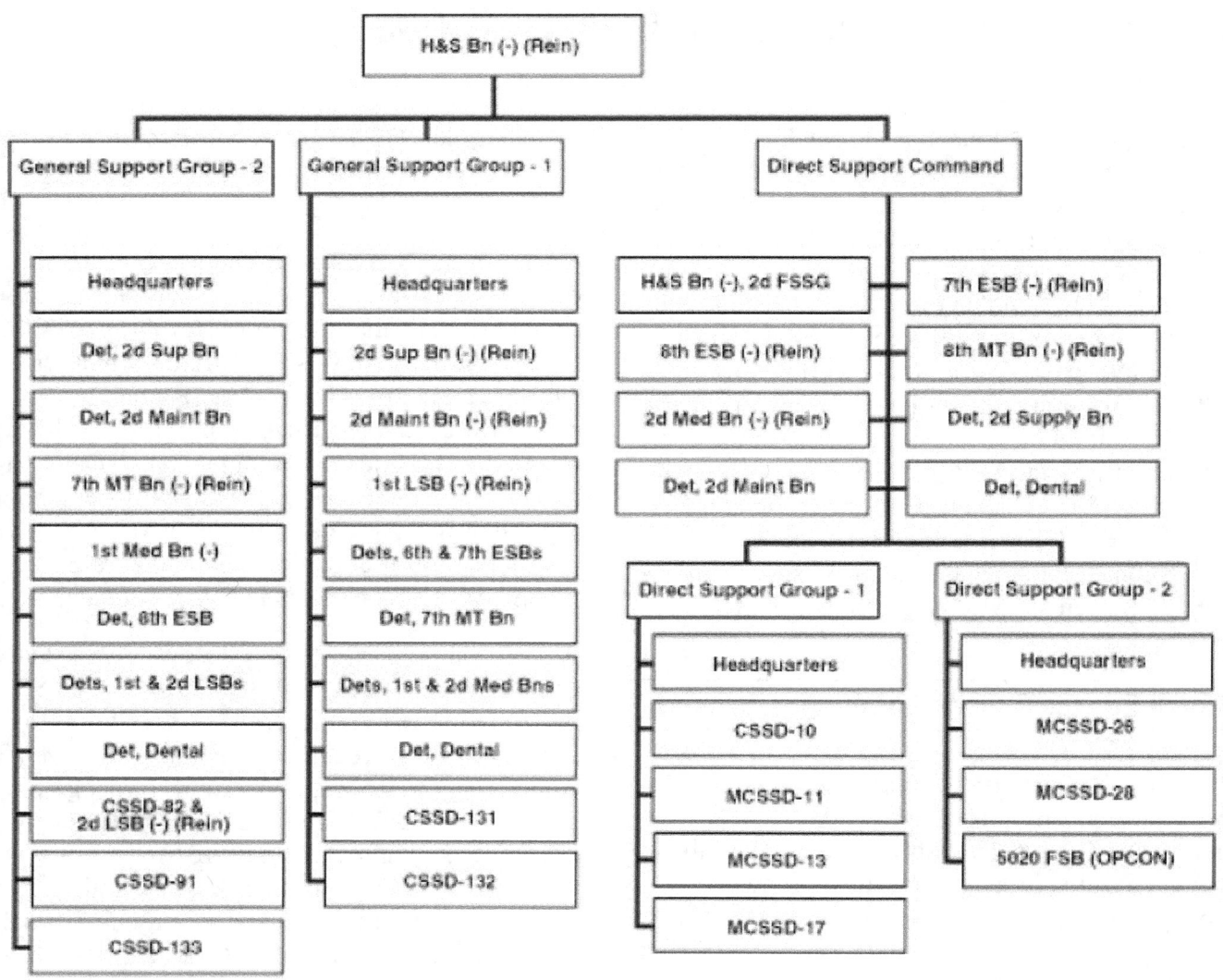

Figure 5-1. 1st FSSG Task Organization for Desert Storm.

requirements. For example, this coordination culminated in the DS command controlling the motor transportation battalions of both FSSGs during the offensive, while the 1st FSSG employed GSG-1 and GSG-2 to conduct operational-level, intratheater lift operations with contracted vehicles, coalition and reserve drivers, and Army tanker trucks.

The MARFOR provides logistic policy and the MLC executes that policy to support forces assigned to the MARFOR. When priorities of support are required, the MARFOR ensures the MLC receives assistance and resources beyond its organic capabilities. The MAGTF submits its requirements to the MLC, which analyzes the requirements for supportability.

Mission

The MLC is a CSSE designated as the MARFOR operational logistic unit. The CSSE deploys to establish the MARFOR logistic support structure to facilitate force closure operations, including arrival and assembly. On order redesignated as the

MLC, the CSSE provides GS to MARFOR and other assigned and/or attached forces to ensure the forward warfighting focus of the MAGTF.

Deployment Criteria

FSSG commanders should task-organize to accomplish DS, GS, and operational-level support missions. When confronted with the following criteria, the MARFOR should consider employing a CSSE as an MLC:

- Theater logistic support is shallow or has short-falls.
- Common item or user logistics is planned.
- Expeditious force closure of a MEB or larger is anticipated.
- A MEB or larger will be ashore more than 60 days.
- Sequential MPF offloads or back loads are planned.

Tasks

The MLC creates and/or integrates existing and emerging theater support systems. The MLC receives, stores, fixes, and moves logistics in GS of the MAGTF. It manages the continual flow of logistics in and out of theater. Force closure operations are critical, since they facilitate the operational standup of the MAGTF. During operations, the MLC provides tactical and operational-level support.

As the tactical situation requires, the MLC employs detachments and continues to organize theater support. If CSSEs of the MAGTF have been executing operational logistic tasks, the MLC relieves them. The MLC supports MAGTFs assigned to other components, such as an amphibious MAGTF assigned or attached to the NCC. Even when a MAGTF stays afloat, the MLC assists with maintenance, equipment replacement, supply support, etc. The MLC should be mobile enough to reduce the logistic risk to the MAGTF by moving elements close to the combat zone and shortening the length of LOC. As directed, the MLC supports multina-

tional and other Service forces, but is not a joint or multinational theater logistic force. The MLC performs the following tasks:

- Establishes an intertheater and intratheater logistic system.
- Coordinates arrival and assembly and other force closure operations.
- Provides operational-level logistics.
- Integrates HNS, inter-Service, common item, and cross-service support as directed by the CINC.
- Develops logistic requirements in conjunction with the MARFOR.

Employment Considerations

An effective MLC must conduct operations that facilitate MAGTF force closure and build a foundation for the emerging logistic system. This system can be built incrementally to support the surge requirements of the MAGTF during force closure and initial tactical operations. After the theater logistic system is established, the MLC pulls sustainment from the strategic base to meet MAGTF requirements and facilitate reconstitution and redeployment operations. In creating the conditions for MAGTF success, the MLC integrates MAGTF requirements with intertheater and intratheater logistic systems. The MLC normally operates within the theater COMMZ and provides the means to extend the MAGTF operational reach.

Force Closure

The MLC arrives in theater and initiates actions to establish the MARFOR logistic distribution system. The MLC establishes and operates an MCC, port operations groups (POGs) and/or beach operations groups (BOGs), and arrival airfield control groups (AACGs). Table 5-1 on page 5-4 provides a possible division of labor between the MLC and the MAGTF CSSE for arrival and assembly operations. The MARFOR, in coordination with its major subordinate commands, establishes the division of labor for an actual contingency or operation.

Table 5-1. Division of Labor for Force Closure.

Functional Area	MAGTF CSSE Responsibilities	MLC Responsibilities
Arrival and assembly operations	Off-loads MPSRON first.	Employs subsequent MPF, MAGTF, and follow-on sustainment.
Throughput plan	Plans initial movement to assembly areas.	Plans for throughput of MAGTF and other follow-on MARFOR. Develops LOC requirements in support of MARFOR.
MCC	Establishes and operates initial capability.	Assumes responsibility for MCC coordination with theater MCC once MAGTF moves out from assembly areas. Provides movement control on LOC under the Marine component's supervision.
POG/BOG	Establishes and operates for initial MPSRON off load.	Assumes responsibility once MAGTF moves out from assembly areas. Opens new ports and beach support areas required to support MARFOR.
Airfield/departure air control group	Establishes and operates initial capability for MAGTF arrival.	Assumes responsibility once MAGTF moves out from assembly areas. Opens new airfields required to support MARFOR.
Arrival and assembly operations group (AAOG)	Serves as lead agent for MAGTF arrival and assembly.	Executes AAOG responsibilities under MARFOR direction when MAGTF AAOG is disestablished.
Materials handling equipment (MHE) Plan	Supports initial MAGTF arrival.	Develops for sustainment operations.
ITV	Provides ITV within the MAGTF.	Provides ITV between MAGTF and outside sources.
Maritime pre-positioned equipment and supplies (MPE/S) distribution plan	Plans initial MPF arrival and assembly.	Plans subsequent MPF, MAGTF, and follow-on sustainment.
C2	Initial MPF arrival and assembly, MAGTF operations.	Coordinates support for MARFOR with theater and strategic support organizations.
Fly-in echelon	Monitors initial MPF arrival and assembly.	Monitors subsequent MPF, MAGTF, and follow-on sustainment.
Arrival and assembly operations element (AAOE)	Directs/coordinates initial MPF arrival and assembly.	Directs/coordinates subsequent MPF, MAGTF, and follow-on sustainment.

Because of initial force closure efforts, the MLC establishes a forward base for sustained operations. The MLC supports the arrival and assembly of subsequent MPFs, the force closure of the MAGTF follow-on echelon, and intratheater and intertheater sustainment operations. The MLC coordinates Marine force closure activities with the JFC and joint movement control agencies.

Contracting personnel should be included in the MLC to initiate contingency contracting operations resulting from emergency requirements, and to establish relations with local vendors. When authorized by the MARFOR, MLC contractors coordinate activities with joint agencies. Legal service support and civil affairs personnel assist in host nation relations, contracting, and obtain-

ing HNS and liaison with joint agencies that manage these functions.

During force closure, MLC coordinates construction requirements include building camps, medical facilities, bulk fuel and water storage sites, and ammunition storage points; improving existing airfields; and/or establishing forward operating bases. The MLC engineer officer executes MARFOR construction priorities by coordinating the engineering efforts of the MLC, NCF, and MAGTF and coordinates construction projects with the MARFOR engineer officer. The HSS medical coordination cell coordinates the establishment of the HSS system with the MARFOR surgeon, MAGTF surgeon, and the MPF fleet hospitals. The MLC may establish a Marine logistic operations center for C2 of operations modeled after an FSSG-level combat service support operations center.

Sustainment

At ports and airfields, MLC supply personnel receive, store, and prepare MAGTF accompanying supplies for movement to the combat zone. MLC transportation units move cargo and bulk liquids to MAGTF combat service support areas (CSSAs). In addition, the MLC uses contract and other Service trucks, watercraft, and aircraft to move cargo and personnel. MLC engineers may support MAGTF engineers in building ammunition supply points (ASPs), CSSAs, LOCs, and expeditionary airfields. The MLC may establish detachments at MAGTF forward operating bases to provide GS.

To establish a Marine Corps logistic distribution system, the MLC continues to integrate MARFOR activities and requirements with joint agencies per MARFOR guidance. MLC throughput activities are integrated with joint reception, staging, onward movement, and integration (JRSOI), and the activities of the MARFOR MCC are synchronized with JMC operations.

Construction projects focus on expanding warehouses and maintenance facilities and on maintaining and improving intratheater LOC and throughput infrastructure. The MLC solidifies and improves common item, inter-Service, and host nation support with providers. If required, MLC assists amphibious MAGTFs. The MLC plans reconstitution and redeployment with an emphasis on MPF regeneration operations.

To sustain the MAGTF, the MLC synchronizes resupply based on MARFOR priorities and policies, joint stockage levels, and buildup rates. To prevent bottlenecks, the MLC uses its central position to pull supplies into theater in time to deliver them to the MAGTF. The MLC uses demand input from the MAGTF CSSEs and the capabilities of the theater distribution system to focus on the most demanding logistic tasks facing

the MARFOR. Use of MLC transportation assets and HNS assets in the combat zone adds responsiveness and flexibility to logistic support for the MAGTF. See appendix A for a notional functional division of labor between the MARFOR, MLC, and FSSG.

Reconstitution

Although reconstitution is largely a command and operations function, the actual refitting, supply, personnel fill, and medical actions are conducted by CSS and administrative elements, such as MLC. The MLC begins reconstitution planning before the employment phase of the expeditionary operation. The MLC obtains and analyzes the MAGTF projection for reconstitution requirements, participates in the planning process, and coordinates Marine Corps requirements with joint agencies and strategic organizations. MLC planning and executing actions include the following:

● Determining the MAGTF resource requirements.
● Coordinating Marine Corps requirements with joint, host nation, and strategic logistic support agencies.
● Synchronizing the recovery of the MAGTF from the combat zone with the tactical situation.
● Synchronizing reconstitution and redeployment operations with theater and strategic lift.
● Establishing maintenance areas, parking and staging areas, and warehousing.
● Designating, organizing, and establishing procedures for washdown sites.
● Staging shipping containers, packaging, and dunnage for redeployment.
● Arranging customs, agricultural, and other pre-redeployment inspections.
● Maintaining the continuity of operations between MPF regeneration and other reconstitution.

There are two methods of conducting reconstitution—reorganization and regeneration. Reorganization is action taken to shift internal resources within a degraded unit to increase its level of combat effectiveness. Regeneration is action taken to reconstitute a unit through significant replacement of personnel, equipment, and supplies in an attempt to restore a unit to full operational capability as rapidly as possible.

Reorganization

Normally completed at the unit level, reorganization does not require extensive external support. Reorganization is normally limited to the replenishment, repair, and potential redistribution of assets within a unit for a follow-on mission.

Regeneration

Regeneration returns the force to pre-employment levels of readiness. Normally, regeneration is accomplished by the MEF or MARFOR and involves augmentation from the SE. Regeneration requires additional resources, coordination, and operational planning, to include movement and training plans to recover the unit's combat effectiveness.

When established, the MLC, augmented by the SE, will be the executor of regeneration operations. Per MARFOR direction, the MLC will manage the inbound replacement equipment and combat replacement companies. The MLC will provide storage for equipment and billeting for personnel. In addition, MLC will coordinate movement of personnel and equipment to major subordinate commands based on MARFOR priorities. When an MLC is not established, MARFOR will plan movement of replacement personnel and equipment from outside the theater directly to the major subordinate commands.

Maritime Pre-positioning Force Operations

MPF is a capability for expeditious force closure in theaters of operations bordering the sea. MPF and amphibious operations are complementary capabilities. The Marine Corps and the Navy have developed tactics, techniques, and proce-

dures for MPF force closure and regeneration operations. These procedures are published in Naval Warfare Publication (NWP) 22-10/Fleet Marine Force Manual 1-5, *Maritime Prepositioning Force (MPF) Operations*.

Arrival and Assembly

Arrival and assembly operations occur in a permissive or uncertain environment and terminate when the MAGTF commander reports that the MPF MEB is combat ready. Operations occur in an AAA. The AAA is an administrative area that includes airfields, port facilities, beaches, transportation, and distribution networks. An establishing authority (e.g., CINC, JFC, Service component commander, or a subordinate naval commander) designates an AAA. The AAOG controls arrival and assembly operations through a network of subordinate control organizations.

Arrival and Assembly Operations Group

The AAOG is a task-organized group from the MPF MAGTF CE that coordinates and controls arrival and assembly operations. It consists of personnel from all MAGTF elements plus liaison from the Navy support element. The AAOG's subordinate elements are the landing force support party (LFSP), MCC, and AAOEs. The AAOG monitors the airflow of the fly-in echelon into the AAA; coordinates the throughput and distribution of equipment and supplies from the MPSs to the unit assembly areas; and provides initial C2 functions for the MAGTF in the AAA.

Landing Force Support Party

The LFSP controls throughput of personnel and MPE/S at theater ports, beaches, and airfields. In addition, the LFSP facilitates CSS ashore during ship-to-shore movement in amphibious operations. For MPF operations, the LFSP has four elements: POG, BOG, an arrival/departure airfield control group (A/DACG), and an MCC.

Port Operations Group. A task-organized group of Navy cargo-handling forces from the BSSG, the POG—

- Prepares the port before the arrival of the MPF.
- Unloads ships.
- Controls the throughput of offloaded supplies and equipment.

Beach Operations Group. The BOG is a task-organized group from the Navy support element and the BSSG. The BOG is responsible for preparing the beach before the arrival of the MPSRON and the throughput of supplies and equipment after the ships are offloaded.

Arrival/Departure Airfield Control Group. The A/DACG is responsible for controlling and coordinating the off-load and onload of airfield units and equipment and providing limited CSS to those units. Task-organized around a nucleus provided by the landing support element of the BSSG, A/DACG is structured and manned to provide continuous operations support for multiple aircraft.

Movement Control Center. The MCC is the agency that plans, routes, schedules, and controls personnel and equipment movements over LOC. In MPF operations at ports, airfields, and/or beaches, the MCC forms convoys containing MPE/S and personnel and dispatches them to the AAOEs.

Arrival and Assembly Operations Element. Established by each element of the MAGTF and Navy support element, the AAOE receives MPE/S and distributes the equipment to units of the MAGTF.

Regeneration

Regeneration is the reconstitution method used to restore the MPF to full operational capability as rapidly as possible upon completion of the MAGTF's employment mission. The combatant commander, in consultation with MARFOR, determines the operational capability of the regenerated MPF. Regeneration occurs in the following stages:

- Actions in the AOR during MAGTF operations.
- Actions in the AOR following the MAGTF operations.
- MPF maintenance cycle at BIC.

The regeneration of an MPF is most effectively accomplished at BIC in Florida. However, the need to obtain operational capabilities quickly can dictate that regeneration be initiated in the theater of operations and later completed at BIC. Planning for regeneration is extensive, much of which occurs at the strategic level. Figure 5-2 depicts the organizations involved with planning and executing the regeneration of the MPF.

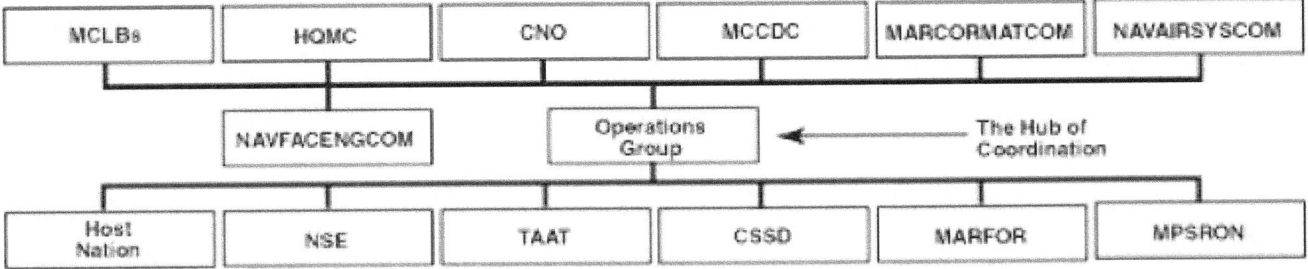

Figure 5-2. MPF Regeneration Organizations.

Marine Corps Forces

The MARFOR has extensive responsibilities for regenerating an MPF. One of the main participants in the regenerating process, MARFOR controls the CSSD and TAAT, recommends the deferment of the regeneration in the theater of operations, and decides to load the MPF based on conditions in theater. The MARFOR has the following planning actions and responsibilities for regenerating the MPF:

- Recommend the primary regeneration site to the establishing authority.
- Participate in drafting applicable orders, plans, and letters of instruction.
- Publish guidance for the return of MPE/S, to include shipping containers, original packaging, dunnage, and the assignment of designated staging areas.
- Review the redeployment plan for conflict with the regeneration plan. (The redeployment plan should support the regeneration plan, to include security considerations.)
- Provide instructions for the security, inventory, and condition coding of MPE/S.
- Establish priorities for acquisition, performance of equipment maintenance, and preparation of supplies.
- Designate, organize, and establish procedures for washdown sites.
- Establish maintenance areas, parking and staging areas, and warehousing.
- Implement logistic information systems supporting accountability and prepositioning database management.
- Establish priorities for use of high usage equipment and assets.
- Identify how the MAGTF's mission and organic T/E requirements may affect regeneration.
- Develop procedures to ensure MPE/S meets United States Department of Agriculture inspection standards before loading.
- Arrange for a senior agricultural inspection team.

Technical Assistance Advisory Team

The TAAT is comprised of military and civilian personnel from MCLBs to provide a nucleus of expertise for the MPF regeneration. Normally, personnel from BIC staff the TAAT and are either OPCON or tactical control to the MARFOR.

Combat Service Support Element

A CSSE (MLC if established) will be assigned as the MARFOR's executive agent for regeneration. Task-organized with personnel from the theater and continental United States (CONUS), CSSE is focused on the regeneration of the MPF. The CSSE is responsible for early planning, CSSA establishment, and MPE/S maintenance during MAGTF operations.

Navy Support Element

During MPF regeneration, Navy support element supplies and equipment are regenerated. The Navy support element is composed of naval beach group staff and subordinate unit personnel, a detachment of Navy cargo-handling personnel, and other Navy capabilities, as required. The regeneration of the Navy support element should be accomplished with assistance from the NCC in cooperation with the MARFOR.

Theater Movement Control Operations

Theater movement control consists of the planning, routing, scheduling, controlling common-user assets, and maintaining ITV. In theater, either joint, Service, or multinational movement control organizations conduct movement control.

Joint

In a joint environment, movement control coordinates transportation resources to enhance combat effectiveness and meet the priorities of the commander. The combatant commander may direct a subordinate JFC and the Service components to perform their own movement control. The combatant commander may establish a theater JMC and/or JTB. To ensure transportation system requirements are fully integrated, the combatant commander may assign responsibility to a single joint office, the JMC.

Joint Movement Center

The JMC is responsible for coordinating the employment of transportation to support the theater concept of operations. The JMC establishes theater transportation policies relative to need, port and terminal capabilities, transportation asset availability, and the JFC's priorities. The JMC can be the single coordinator of strategic movements with USTRANSCOM. Figure 5-3 depicts a notional JMC organization. To coordinate transportation employment and policies, the JMC—

- Interfaces with JOPES to monitor and regulate the deployment of forces and supplies.
- Analyzes user capabilities to ship, receive, handle cargo, and recommend solutions to shortfalls.
- Advises the J-4 on transportation matters that would adversely affect combat contingency operations.

- Serves as the liaison with the host nation(s) for transportation issues.
- Disseminates information concerning host nation transportation systems, facilities, equipment, and personnel.

Joint Transportation Board

The JTB is an ad hoc board that makes prioritized recommendations to the commander. The geographic combatant commander may establish a theater JTB to review and deconflict policies, priorities, and transportation apportionment beyond the authority of the JMC.

The JTB is generally comprised of the senior logisticians from the participating Services as voting members and other subject matter experts as needed in advisory roles. The JTB consists of representatives from the Service components, movement control agencies, and combatant command J-3 (operations), J-4 (logistics), and J-5 (plans). Normally, the J-4 chairs the JTB, which requests additional transportation assets from the Joint Chiefs of Staff (JCS) when intratheater assets do not support the combatant commander's concept of operation. When there is no theater JTB, the JMC is the primary advisor to the JFC.

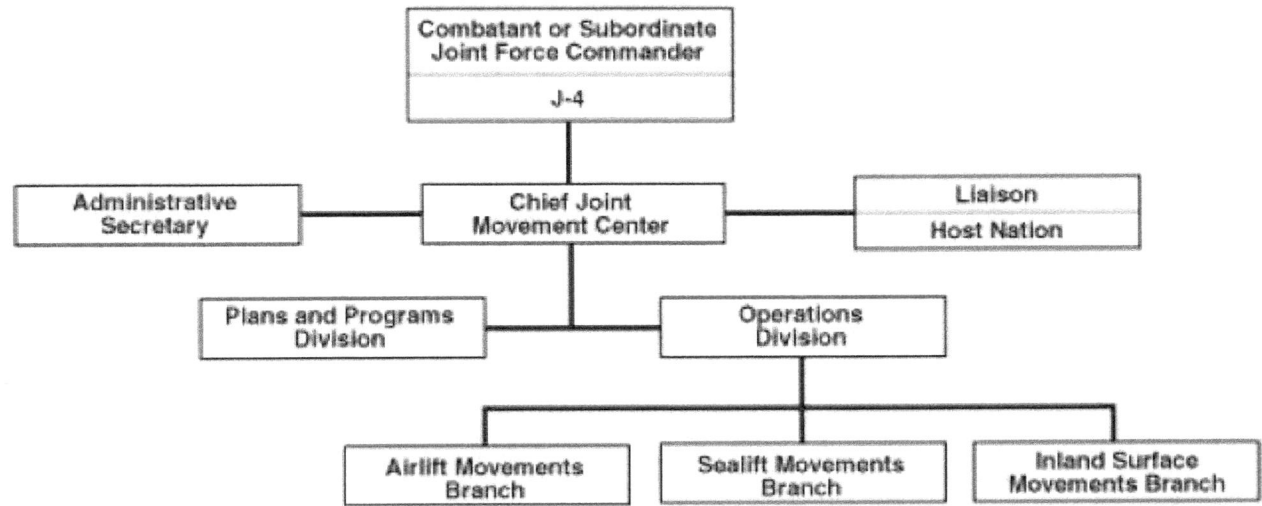

Figure 5-3. Suggested JMC Organization.

Requirements

The JMC plans, apportions, allocates, coordinates, and deconflicts transportation, as well as establishes and operates an ITV system to assist tracking theater movements of units, personnel, unit equipment, and materiel.

Planning. The JMC develops the theater movement plan that supports the JFC's priorities and concept of operations. The plan must synchronize incoming strategic movements with theater reception and onward movement operations.

Apportioning. Transportation apportionment is usually expressed in percentages, developed in cycles, and supports the combatant commander's concept of operations. In transportation apportionment decisions, JMC must consider the mission, resources available, threat, and geography of the AOR. Components use the transportation apportionment decision for transportation allocation and employment.

Allocating. Allocating is the assignment of specific transportation resources against specific movement missions. If a JMC is not established, the geographic combatant commander usually delegates the transportation allocation process to the Service components. Components normally express transportation allocations as sorties by type of aircraft, gross tonnage, number of vehicles, or other appropriate terms. If a JMC is established, Service components work with the JMC to optimize daily movements based on projected daily transportation resources available.

Coordinating. The JMC coordinates common-user theater air, land, and sea transportation. The JMC initially coordinates common-user transportation through the movement plan, monitors the transportation system, analyzes movement performance, and prepares adjustments. In addition, the JMC coordinates the fulfillment of requirements forwarded by component control elements. Implementation of adjustments occurs during the development of priorities or the scheduling of assets. The JMC approves unit surface movements that use common-user assets and main supply routes.

Deconflicting. The JMC deconflicts theater transportation requirements. Deconflicting requirements involves establishing and managing the transportation request process. It includes validating requests and tasking appropriate transportation assets. Transportation requirements that cannot be deconflicted by the JMC are forwarded to the JTB for resolution.

Force Tracking. The JMC provides the geographic combatant commander the ability to locate units that are using common-user transport within the theater. The JMC can monitor the inland surface movement of forces during theater movements, such as documenting arrivals at aerial ports of debarkation (APODs)/seaports of debarkation (SPODs) and movements to intermediate staging areas or to final tactical assembly areas (TAAs).

Multinational

An MNFC may establish a TMCC to coordinate and control movement into and out of theater and to provide visibility over movement requirements. During termination and redeployment, the TMCC ensures smooth redeployment according to the established redeployment plan. The TMCC coordinates, deconflicts, and integrates inbound and outbound strategic lift with the intratheater movement requirements. The TMCC is integrated with national and geographic MCCs.

Marine Corps Forces

Movement control procedures were developed to help MAGTFs move expeditiously from their home stations and bases to ports and airfields of embarkation, and subsequently from debarkation points through reception areas and on to their destinations. Movement control coordinates a complex operation that involves Marine Corps tactical units, bases and stations, ports, airfields, contracted transportation, and strategic sealift and airlift. In addition, movement control procedures are applicable for coordinating and controlling intratheater lift. Figure 5-4 depicts theater movement control focused on the MARFOR. The movement control group, FMCC, logistic movement control center (LMCC), and unit movement control center (UMCC) perform movement control and coordination functions.

Movement Control Group

This is the MARFOR commander's optional agency to coordinate intertheater and intratheater lift. Normally, the MLC establishes the movement control group, which coordinates with USTRANSCOM through the JMC for strategic lift and with the JMC for theater movement control.

Force Movement Control Center

The FMCC is the MAGTF commander's agency to control and coordinate deployment support

activities. This agency coordinates and schedules the MAGTF's strategic lift requirements through the movement control group.

Logistic Movement Control Center

The LMCC is operated by the FSSG/CSSE. It reports to the FMCC and coordinates the execution of movement based on FMCC priorities. The LMCC provides transportation, transportation scheduling, MHE, and other support to units before they move. It coordinates transportation and MHE requirements with tactical units, other Services, and/or the host nation.

Unit Movement Control Center

The major subordinate commands of the MAGTF establish UMCCs, which are the unit nodes in the movement control system. UMCCs control the transportation and communications assets needed

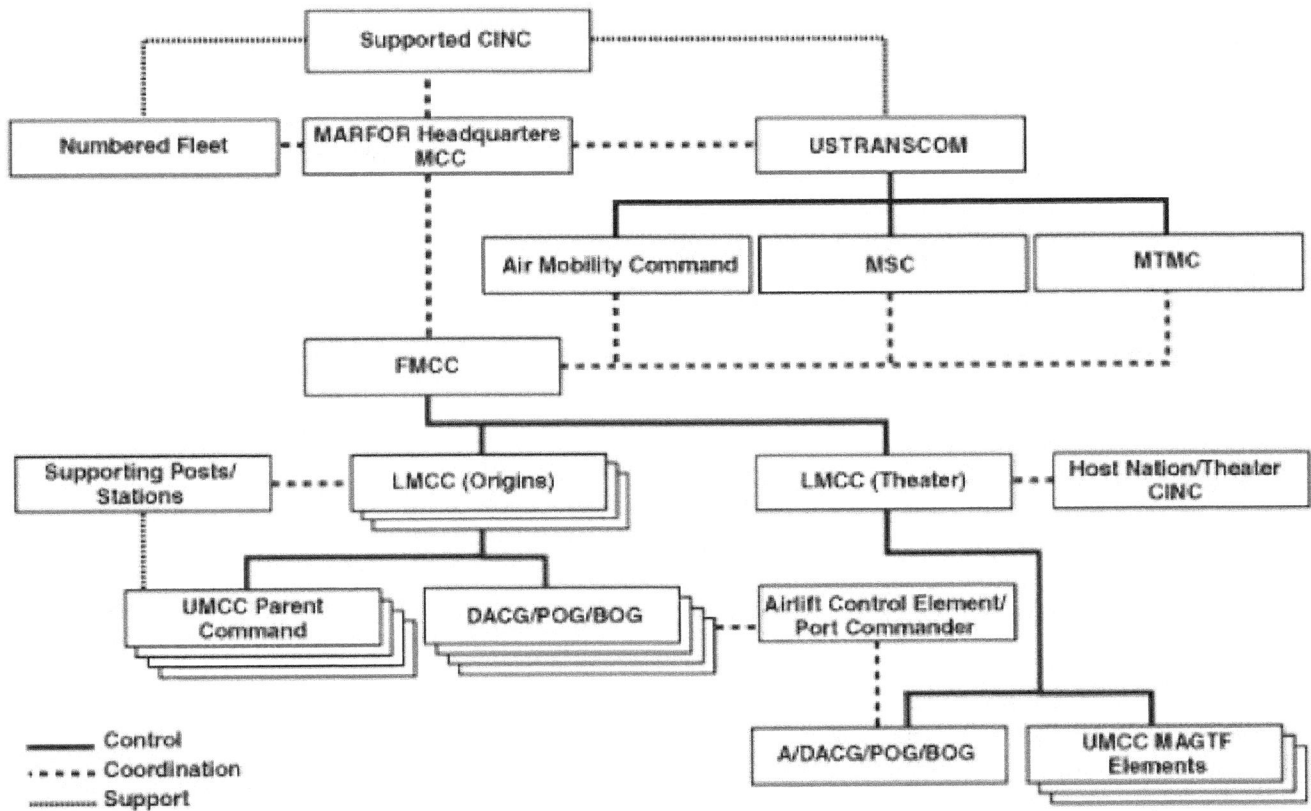

Figure 5-4. Theater Movement Control.

to execute the deployment of their units. They coordinate their needs with the LMCC.

Joint and Multinational Logistic Operations

The JFC's requirement for effective and efficient logistic operations has stimulated the development of joint operations for JRSOI, JLOTS, Service support, and HSS support.

Joint Reception, Staging, Onward Movement, and Integration

JRSOI is a joint force closure operation that processes and prepares personnel, equipment, and materiel arriving in a theater of war.

Process

The JFC may direct that components of a joint force participate in the following JRSOI process when entering a theater of war:

- Reception operations include functions required to receive and clear unit personnel, equipment, and materiel through the ports of debarkation.
- Staging is the process of organizing arriving personnel, equipment, and materiel into units and forces.
- Onward movement is the process of moving units and accompanying materiel from reception facilities, marshalling areas, and staging areas to TAAs or other theater destinations.
- Integration is the synchronized handoff of units into an operational commander's force before mission execution. Efforts focus on preparing for future operations and integrating into the joint force.

Participating Organizations

JRSOI is the responsibility of the supported combatant commander who receives the forces. The success of JRSOI is dependent on the cooperation of the following participating organizations:

- Supporting combatant commanders.
- JTF commanders.
- Service component commanders.
- Deploying units.
- Allies.
- Host nations.
- Contractors.
- Support organizations (enabling units, supporting combatant commanders).

Command and Control

Supported combatant commanders and their subordinates should be flexible in modifying command structures to meet the specific requirements of each situation with emphasis on unity of effort, whether it be a small humanitarian operation or an MTW. The combatant commander may employ the following options for the C2 of JRSOI.

Existing J-4 Staff. The JFC augments the existing J-4 staff with sufficient assets to exercise both staff planning and operational supervision over JRSOI.

Joint Command and Control Early Entry Force. The JFC may deploy a joint C2 early entry force to provide the initial JRSOI management and coordination capability. This joint force provides the initial C2 for the theater and forms the nucleus of the joint command.

Most Capable Service. The combatant commander may assign JRSOI responsibilities to the Service component most capable of performing the mission.

Dominant User. The combatant commander assigns responsibility for providing or coordinating JRSOI support to the Service component that is the primary consumer.

Service Responsibility. Each Service is responsible for its own force closure or RSOI of individuals, equipment, and supplies.

Joint Logistics Over-the-Shore

JLOTS operations are logistics over-the-shore (LOTS) operations conducted by two or more Services, ordinarily involving the Army, Navy, and Marine Corps. The operations are LOTS when only one Service is involved. LOTS/JLOTS operations occur when there is a requirement to load and unload ships without adequate port facilities in either friendly or undefended territory. Conducted over unimproved shorelines and through inadequate ports, LOTS/JLOTS operations rely on barges, causeways, crane ships, and offshore petroleum discharge systems to move cargo and fuel from ship to shore and onward to inland marshalling and staging areas.

Service Support

Although logistics is a Service responsibility, the Marine Corps can receive support from other Services. Service support is either received from or provided to other Services in all theaters and for all types of operations; or it is associated with a specific theater, OPLAN, or situation. In addition to the responsibilities that apply in all theaters and for all Services, a JFC may designate a Service, usually the dominant user or most capable Service, to provide common item/service support for the entire theater, areas within a theater or specific operations.

The Army has been designated as the executive agent responsible for certain support functions in all theaters. The Army provides management of overland petroleum support to U.S. land-based forces of DOD components. Responsible for inland distribution during wartime, the Army provides the necessary force structure to construct, operate, and maintain an inland petroleum distribution system. In an undeveloped theater, the Army also provides a system that transports bulk petroleum inland from the high-water mark of the designated ocean beach. The Army is normally responsible for providing the other Services with the following theater distribution support:

- Veterinary service support.
- Single integrated medical logistics management (SIMLM).
- Controlled disposal of waste, explosives, and munitions.
- Mortuary affairs.
- Military troop construction support to U.S. Air Force outside the continental United States (OCONUS).
- Executive agency for DOD EPW detainee program.
- Common-user land transportation in overseas areas.
- Intermodal container management.
- Overseas ocean terminal operations.
- Management of military postal services.
- Executive agency for land-based water resources.
- Executive agency for the DOD customs inspection program.
- Management of conventional ammunition.
- Executive agency for processing claims (in selected countries).
- Executive agency for settlement of tort claims by DOD employees.
- Locomotive management.
- Single manager for military traffic management.
- Food safety service.
- Overland petroleum support management.
- Inland logistics support to the Marine Corps.
- Executive agency for AIT.

Theater Health Service Support

Service components are responsible for establishing HSS systems; however, the JFC may direct the integration of HSS in a theater of war. The MARFOR is responsible for coordinating and integrating HSS within its AOR. The Marine component surgeon, dental officer, medical planner, and medical administrative officer advise the MARFOR commander on matters relating to the health of the command such as sanitation, disease surveillance, medical intelligence, medical logistics, patient movement, and medical personnel issues. The

MARFOR surgeon serves as liaison to the JFS. Appendix A provides a notional division of labor for HSS. The MARFOR, in coordination with its major subordinate commands, will establish the division of labor for the actual contingency or operation. Theater HSS includes the joint theater HSS system, JFS, health service logistic support, theater blood management, intratheater patient movement, and multinational HSS.

Joint Theater Heath Service Support System

In a theater of war, health care is provided by level. Each level reflects an increase in medical capability while retaining the capabilities found in the preceding level. Within most theaters of operations, there are four levels of care. See figure 5-5.

The MAGTF can provide care at levels I and II but receives external support for levels II through IV from the Navy and the other Services. To support the Marines, the Navy designates amphibious shipping as casualty receiving and treatment ships (CRTS) for level II and III support and

deploys hospital ships and fleet hospitals for levels III and IV. The MPF program includes a fleet hospital in each MPS, which provides the MARFOR a level III MTF. The Army and Air Force also deploy level III and IV capabilities to the theater of operations. Figure 5-6 illustrates theater medical capabilities.

Joint Force Surgeon

The combatant commander designates a JFS to be responsible for preparing and coordinating HSS within a joint force. The JFS section should be staffed by members representing all Services and be of sufficient size to effectively perform the following tasks:

- Joint coordination of HSS initiatives.
- Regionalization.
- Standardization and interoperability.
- Development of the HSS plan.
- Review of subordinate plans and operations.
- Medical resupply.

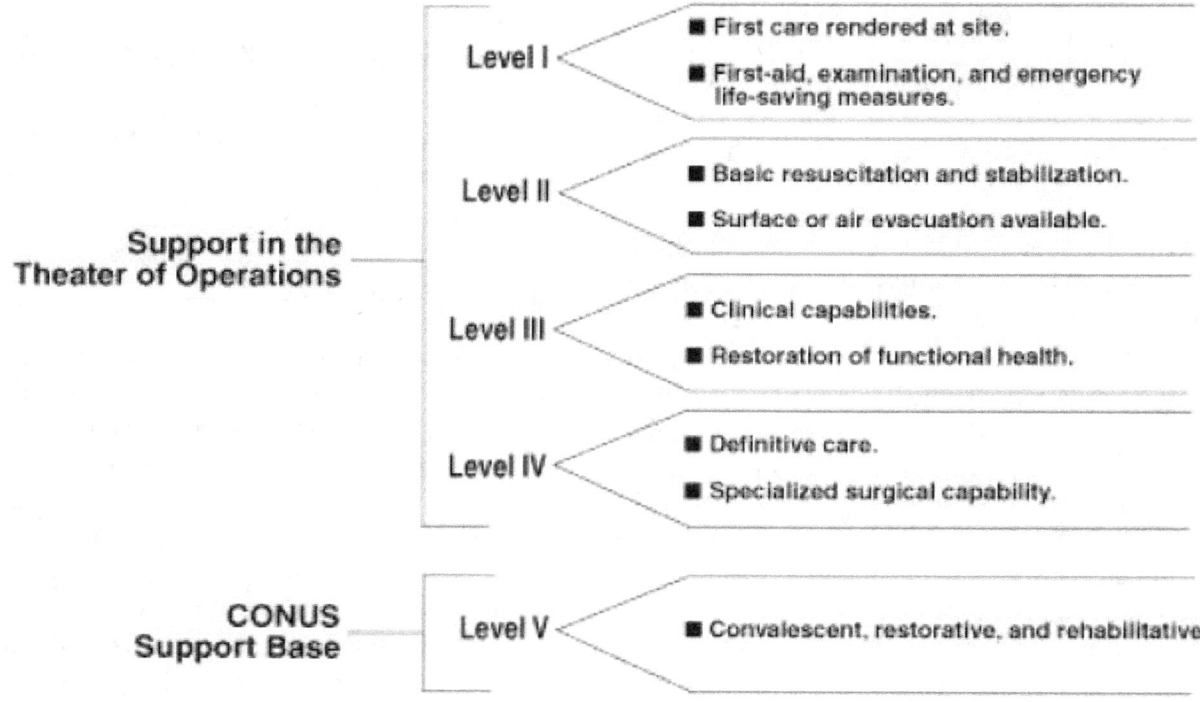

Figure 5-5. HSS Levels.

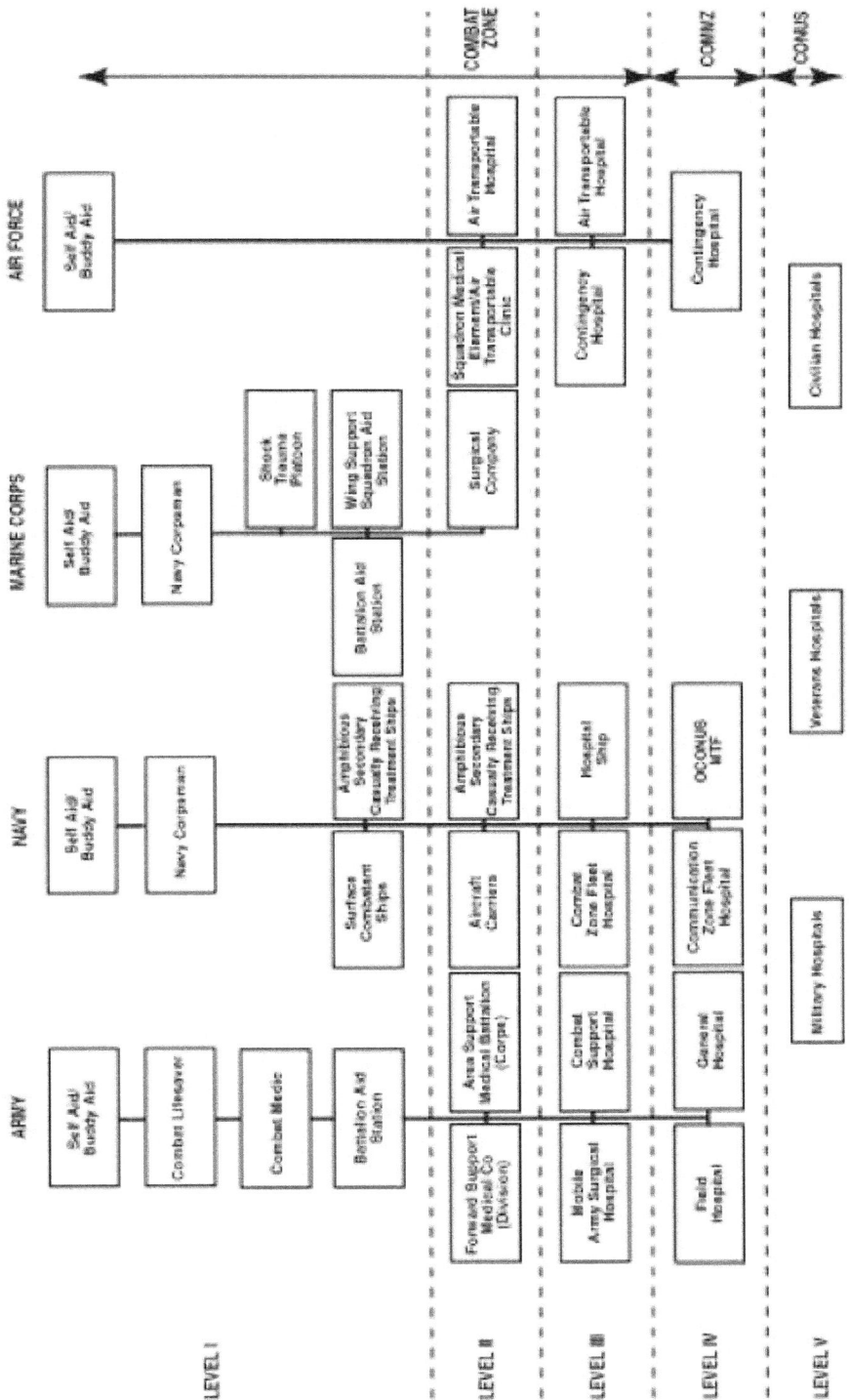

Figure 5-6. Theater Medical Capabilities.

Logistic Support

The Service components are responsible for providing health service logistic support to their forces. Every MAGTF deploys with a tailored block of accompanying medical supplies to support the force for a predetermined number of days. However, the combatant commander may exercise directive authority over medical logistics and appoint the dominant user and/or most capable service as a SIMLM to coordinate theater medical logistics.

The SIMLM is responsible for the provision of medical supplies, medical equipment maintenance and repair, blood management, and optical fabrication to joint forces within the theater of operations including, on emergency basis, Navy ships for common-use items.

In the European and Korean theaters, the U.S. Army is the designated SIMLM. The JFC may designate the ASCC as the SIMLM in future operations because of its probable role as dominant user. However, the combatant commander may designate either the Navy or Air Force components as the SIMLM when either organization is the dominant user and/or the most capable Service.

Theater Blood Management

MAGTF level II MTFs and MPF fleet hospitals require blood to care for injured personnel. The JBPO plans, coordinates, and directs the handling, storage, and distribution of blood and blood components within the AOR. For a comprehensive description of blood management in support of MARFOR, see MCWP 4-11.1, *Health Service Support Operations*.

Intratheater Patient Movement

Intratheater patient movement agencies use theater resources to evacuate patients to and between medical MTFs. Patient movement requires a coordinated effort between Service components, host nation, and theater evacuation assets. The JFS is responsible for developing intratheater patient movement policies in coordination with Service component evacuation representatives.

Tactical commands are responsible for patient evacuation from point of injury to level I patient treatment stations and patient movement from level I to level II. Patient movement within and from level II is normally the responsibility of the senior medical regulating authority in theater. When this is not possible, use of common-user theater AE aircraft for the movement of patients from level II to level III and beyond is determined by the JFC through the JFS. Some joint operations may present unique situations where a level III medical infrastructure does not exist and stabilized patients may be evacuated directly to a level IV MTF in another theater or CONUS.

Patient movement support of theater medical regulating decisions is accomplished using dedicated (Army/Air Force), preplanned and retrograde (Air Force), opportune or designated (Navy/Marine Corps) airlift and may include the use of ground or waterborne assets. The MARFOR coordinates Marine force patient movements with the TPMRC, AECC, joint patient movement requirements center (JPMRC), and Global Patient Movement Requirements Center (GPMRC). See table 5-2 for theater patient movement responsibilities.

Table 5-2. Theater Patient Movement.

Levels of Treatment	Responsibility
Level I to II	MAGTF
Level II to II	MARFOR (MAGTF)
Level II to III	MARFOR (MAGTF/MLC)
Level III to IV and V	TPMRC/JPMRC

Theater Patient Movement Requirements Center. The JFS controls the TPMRC, which coordinates and controls the intertheater/intratheater movement of patients. The TPMRC generates theater plans and schedules patient movement to MTFs. It communicates patient movements with the AECC and with the Service components responsible for executing the transportation mission. The TPMRC should be collocated with and/or have direct access to theater movement control agencies.

Aeromedical Evacuation Coordination Center. The AECC is a coordination center, within the joint AOC's airlift coordination cell, that monitors AE-related activities. It manages the medical aspects of the AE mission and serves as the net control station for AE communications. In addition, AECC coordinates medical requirements with airlift capability, assigns medical missions to the appropriate AE elements, and monitors patient movement activities.

Joint Patient Movement Requirements Center. The JPMRC performs integrated patient movement tasks for units assigned to a JTF or within the task forces' AOR. The JPMRC should be collocated with and/or have direct access with theater movement control agencies.

Global Patient Movement Requirements Center. The TPMRC and JPMRC coordinate requirements to move patients outside of theater with the GPMRC. The GPMRC is a joint activity reporting directly to USCINCTRANS and is the single manager for the strategic and CONUS regulation and movement of uniformed Service patients.

Multinational Health Service Support

Nations are ultimately responsible for providing HSS to their forces; however, because of the high standard of U.S. military HSS, pressure may exist to designate U.S. Forces as the lead nation for HSS in a multinational operation. When participating in a multinational operation, joint and Service component medical and logistic personnel should be aware of differences in national medical standards, customs, and training requirements. The exchange of blood and blood products between nations is an area of deep concern. The

United States might take a lead nation role in the following areas:

- Class VIII medical support.
- Veterinary services.
- Medical laboratory services.
- Optical fabrication.
- Medical equipment.
- Casualty evacuation (air/ground).

The MNFC may designate a theater surgeon with duties similar to the JFS and establish a MEDCC to coordinate multinational, joint, and multifunctional medical issues. The MEDCC is under the cognizance of the theater surgeon and staffed with skilled HSS practitioners representing the nations involved in the operation. It determines opportunities to rationalize HSS in terms of facilities, individual medical disciplines, and transport. The MEDCC can be established as part of an expanded medical staff under the theater surgeon or as a module within the MJLC.

Small Scale and Short Duration Operations

A JTF or MNF may conduct small-scale and short duration operations. The participating MAGTF is usually a MEU or a SPMAGTF, but sometimes a larger MAGTF may be involved. Because of the short duration of the operation, MAGTFs integrate external operational logistic support systems or obtain support directly from the appropriate MARFOR CONUS units via Navy/Marine Corps communications networks.

As an expeditionary force capable of forcible entry, MAGTFs are often the first to enter a theater of operations. In a mature theater, joint support agencies, cross-Service arrangements, and host nations support agreements exist. A MAGTF may coordinate with the U.S. military element belonging to the country team at the embassy.

This element is known by different names depending upon the country; for example, Joint United States Military Advisory Group and Office of Military Cooperation. Another alternative could be support from the Navy distribution system of ALSS and FLS. In most cases, existing support will be austere.

Military Operations Other Than War

Operational-level logistic organizations in the MARFOR may be required to support humanitarian operations, peacekeeping operations (PKO), and domestic support operations (DSO).

Humanitarian Operations

Dislocated civilian support operations are designed to support the resettlement of refugees and displaced persons. Individual governments make the determination on refugee status and normally provide special protection. Refugees are entitled to special protection because they can no longer avail themselves of the protection of their country of nationality. A displaced person could be a refugee who has not yet attained legal status as a refugee or a war criminal that fled to another country to escape prosecution. The Department of State provides guidance on refugee classifications. Refugee and displaced persons programs include camp administration; care (food, supplies, medical care, and protection); and placement (movement or relocation to other countries, camps, and locations).

Normally, refugee operations will involve a MEU, SPMAGTF, and/or MEB as part of a JTF/MNF and numerous NGOs, the International Red Cross, and the United Nations. The MAGTF commander and staff will usually be dual-hatted as the MARFOR commander and staff.

Refugee influxes can overwhelm local ability to care for the numbers of people involved and they have a high probability of occurring in regions remote from a host nation's economic centers. Under these conditions, operational logisticians

who plan and conduct refugee operations should be aware of the following:

- The MAGTF must resupply early because accompanying supplies may be used to support JTF/MNF and/or refugee operations.
- Long and limited LOC between the COMMZ and the area of refugee operation can be expected.
- External intratheater lift will be required to resupply the MAGTF, supply the refugee population, and move refugees to different locations.
- Emphasis will be on distributing food (provided by NGOs), water, fuel, and medical supplies and on providing medical, engineering, mobile electric power, and water purification services.
- Emphasis will be on common items support within the MNF/JTF.
- Consolidated contingency contracting activities must be established to avoid competition for scarce resources between MNF/JTF and the local population.
- Complex command structure will require greater levels of liaison, communications, cooperation, and patience.

Peacekeeping Operations

As military or paramilitary operations undertaken with the consent of all major belligerents, PKO are designed to monitor and facilitate implementation of an existing truce and to support diplomatic efforts to reach a long-term political settlement. The Foreign Assistance Act authorizes the President to furnish assistance to friendly countries and international organizations involved in PKO and other programs that further U.S. national security interests.

PKO take place following diplomatic negotiations and agreements among the belligerents, the sponsoring organization, and nations that provide the peacekeeping forces. The agreement identifies the size, type, and nationality of the forces and the military operations to be conducted. PKO often involve ambiguous situations requiring the peacekeeping force to deal with extreme tension and violence without becoming a participant. The United Nations has been the most frequent sponsor of international PKO. However, regional organizations—such as the Organization of American States, the Organization of African Unity, and the Arab League—have also acted to prevent, halt or contain conflict in their respective regions.

Normally, PKO involve a MEU, SPMAGTF, and/or MPF as part of a JTF/MNF. The MAGTF commander and staff will usually be dual-hatted as the MARFOR commander and staff. Because of the Marine Corps' ability to respond rapidly to international situations, Marine Corps participation will usually occur during the initial phase of a PKO. The highly political, diplomatic, and tense environment of PKO require that operational logisticians be aware of the following:

- Operational logisticians must arrive early to establish liaison with MNF, JTF, and the host nation to facilitate force closure and sustainment.
- Emphasis will be on force protection during intratheater lift and redeployment activities.
- Emphasis will be on the provision of engineer support, class IV construction materiel, and explosive ordnance disposal.
- A greater requirement exists for civil affairs and legal services support on the MARFOR staff.
- The MAGTF must be resupplied early because accompanying supplies may be used to support initial operations of the JTF/MNF forces.
- Directive logistic policy from JTF/MNF headquarters may restrict activities that are normally under the cognizance of component and tactical commanders.
- Emphasis will be on common item support within the JTF/MNF.
- Tight controls on contingency contracting activities must be maintained to avoid competition for resources with the local population and/or to promote goodwill through local purchases.

Domestic Support Operations

DSO include activities and measures taken by DOD to foster mutual assistance and support between the DOD and any civil government agency in planning or preparedness for, or in the application of resources for response to, the consequences of civil emergencies or attacks, including national security emergencies.

Categories

DSO covers a broad array of events that are grouped into two categories:

- Military support to civil authorities (MSCA) is DOD-provided support to civil authorities for domestic emergencies that result from natural or manmade causes. Natural disasters or emergencies include hurricanes, earthquakes, forest fires, and floods. Manmade disasters or emergencies include terrorist attacks, oil spills, radiological contamination, and power outages. Normally, the Federal Emergency Management Agency (FEMA) provides overall coordination of federal consequence management response after a declaration by the President.
- Military support to civilian law enforcement agencies (MSCLEA) includes military assistance for civil disturbances (MACDIS) and other types of support to civilian law enforcement agencies, such as key asset protection and interagency assistance (e.g., training support to law enforcement agencies, support to counterdrug operations, response to weapons of mass destruction, and support for combating terrorism). Normally, the Department of Justice is the lead federal agency for MSCLEA.

Responsibilities

The DOD executive agent for MSCA and MACDIS is the Department of the Army who appoints a director of military support (DOMS) to serve as an action agent. For combating terrorism, the DOMS shares responsibilities with the JCS. Combatant commands have the following geographic or functional responsibilities as DOD's principal DSO planning agents and supported commanders. Table 5-3 lists the combatant commander responsible for each domestic region.

Table 5-3. Combatant Command DSO Responsibilities.

Unified Command	Responsibility
USJFCOM	The 48 contiguous states, the District of Columbia, and U.S. territorial waters.
USSOUTHCOM	Puerto Rico, Virgin Islands, and U.S. territorial waters in the Gulf of Mexico.
USPACOM	Alaska, Hawaii, Guam, the Commonwealth of the Northern Mariana Islands, and U.S. administrative entities and territorial waters.
USTRANSCOM	Single source for transportation to supported combatant commands.
USSOCOM	Combating terrorism incidents involving weapons of mass destruction.

For DSO, the geographic combatant commanders normally establish a JTF by designating an existing command, such as an Army corps, Navy fleet, numbered Air Force or MEF. As with all joint forces, a MARFOR will be assigned to provide logistics and administrative support to MAGTFs serving in a JTF. A SPMAGTF or MEB are the types of MAGTFs most likely to deploy in support of DSO. Joint doctrine for expeditionary operations applies to DSO. Each DSO is situation dependent. Unlike expeditionary operations, DSO occurs in the United States, which facilitates the MARFOR coordination of operational logistic functions.

Considerations

When planning and conducting DSO, operational logisticians should be aware of the following:

• Force closure and redeployment will normally be accomplished through movement control procedures.

• Force protection is a major concern for combating terrorism, counterdrug operations, MACDIS, and essential asset security operations. In other operations, protective measures should be taken to prevent looting and other forms of petty criminal activity by the local populace.

• Sustainment activities may be located near to but outside of the MSCA area, due to transportation bottlenecks and a lack of resources in the disaster area.

• A supporting structure of U.S. military, federal agency, and state and local governmental facilities are usually close to most DSO areas.

• Marine Corps contractors are familiar with procuring goods and services, which are plentiful in the U.S. economy.

• For MSCA operations, emphasis will be on distributing food, water, fuel, and medical supplies and providing medical, engineering, mobile electric power, and water purification support.

• The MARFOR may require civil affairs and legal service augmentation and centralization.

• U.S. law and law enforcement agency procedures will tightly regulate MCLEA support.

CHAPTER 6. STRATEGIC SUPPORT

A central strategic concept in the national military strategy of the United States is power projection. Power projection includes the ability of the Armed Forces of the United States to deploy expeditionary forces to any region in the world and sustain them for missions spanning the operational continuum. U.S. requirements for military force projection include emphasis on rapid deployment of combat power and military operations designed to end conflicts as quickly as possible on terms that are favorable to the United States and its allies.

Crisis response requires the full spectrum of military capabilities, including forcible entry. While the Services include units capable of expeditionary operations, MARFOR are specifically organized, equipped, and trained for expeditionary service. The expeditionary MAGTF is capable of rapid response as part of a naval amphibious force, MPF, or air contingency force. The MAGTF moves to crisis areas via the strategic mobility triad: sealift, pre-positioning, and airlift. The DOD single manager of the DTS is the USTRANSCOM.

Support Organizations

Strategic support organizations include the USTRANSCOM, Department of Transportation, and DLA.

United States Transportation Command

The USCINCTRANS provides air, land, and sea transportation and common-user port management at APODs/SPODs as well as aerial ports of embarkation (APOEs)/seaports of embarkation (SPOEs) for the DOD across the range of military operations. USTRANSCOM is a unified command with transportation component commands (TCCs) from the Air Force's Air Mobility Command (AMC), the Army's MTMC, and the Navy's MSC. The USCINCTRANS commands these components, and the components organize, train, and equip their forces.

USCINCTRANS serves as the DOD single worldwide manager for common-user ports of embarkation and debarkation. As supported commanders, combatant commanders determine movement requirements and required delivery dates, while USTRANSCOM and TCCs provide a complete movement system from origin to initial theater destination. This movement system includes the use of military and commercial assets.

USCINCTRANS has the authority to procure commercial transportation services through component commands and to activate, with approval of the SECDEF, the civil reserve air fleet (CRAF), Ready Reserve Force (RRF), Sealift Readiness Program, and the Voluntary Intermodal Sealift Agreement. The component commands of USTRANSCOM operate the DTS. The specific operations of the DTS are covered in JP 4-01, *Joint Doctrine for the Defense Transportation System.*

USCINCTRANS, through the TCCs (i.e., MTMC, AMC, and MSC), provides strategic air, land, and sea transportation and terminal services to deploy and sustain military forces to meet national security objectives. The TCCs orchestrate a portion of the nation's transportation infrastructure that supports DOD common-user transportation needs.

Military Traffic Management Command

A major Army command, MTMC manages CONUS surface transportation and provides common-use ocean terminal services and traffic management services to deploy, sustain, and redeploy U.S. Forces globally. MTMC conducts transportation engineering to ensure deployability and feasibility of present and future deployment assets. In addition, MTMC is the seaport manager under the single-port manager concept for common-user SPOEs and/or SPODs.

To expeditiously transport troops and materiel to ports of embarkation, railroads, highways, waterways, and a fleet of railcars, buses, trucks, and barges are vital components of the overland lift system. MTMC provides the interface between DOD shippers and the commercial carrier industry. In the United States and overseas, MTMC coordinates force movement to seaports, prepares the ports for ships and cargo, and supervises the loading operations. MTMC manages freight movement in CONUS on surface and air carriers. MTMC operates the defense freight railway interchange fleet of more than 1,000 special use railcars. The command also administers the DOD highways and railroads for national defense programs. MTMC monitors the status of the infrastructure system, including ports, inland waterways, pipelines, and air facilities.

Air Mobility Command

A major Air Force command, AMC provides common-user airlift, air refueling, and strategic AE transportation services to deploy, sustain, and redeploy U.S. Forces globally. In addition, AMC is the single aerial port manager and, where designated, operator of common-user APOEs and/or APODs.

Airlift has the advantage of speed over other modes of transport. AMC's aircraft fleet is composed primarily of airlift aircraft. Another additive force available for long-range airlift in times of national emergency is the CRAF. The CRAF is composed of commercial aircraft committed to support the transportation of military forces and materiel worldwide.

Military Sealift Command

A major Navy command, MSC provides common-user and exclusive-use sealift transportation services to deploy, sustain, and redeploy U.S. Forces globally. MSC provides lift from the sea with a fleet of Government-owned and chartered U.S. flagships that include the following:

- Fast sealift ships—Eight fast sealift ships together can carry the equipment for one Army mechanized or armored division; one of these ships can transport the equivalent of more than 130 C-5 loads of cargo.

- Afloat pre-positioning force—This force includes MPS, pre-positioning ships, and the brigade afloat force.

  o MPS—These 15 ships are divided into three squadrons. Each squadron is within 5-days sailing of potential contingency sites and can support a MEB of 17,600 personnel for 30 days.

  o Pre-positioning ships—These seven ships serve military departments, DLA, and the Defense Fuel Supply Center. Pre-positioning ships are loaded with military equipment and materiel for the Services.

  o Brigade afloat force—Consisting of 14 ships located in Diego Garcia and the Western Pacific, the brigade afloat force is loaded with an Army heavy brigade that is deployable to potential contingency sites in the Middle or Far East within 12 days. Basically floating warehouses, these ships can support 10,000 Army personnel for 15 days.

- Ready Reserve Force—The RRF is a force of ships maintained in a reduced operating status or a layup status by the Maritime Administration for use by DOD in a war or contingency. RRF ships carry combat surge and follow-on cargo. When activated, these ships come under OPCON of MSC. RRF ships are crewed by civilian mariners employed by a Maritime Administration contractor. The MSC-controlled fleet of tankers and dry cargo vessels chartered from the private sector of the U.S. flag shipping industry provide sealift services in areas of the world not normally served by regularly scheduled U.S. flag service.

Department of Transportation

During national defense emergencies, the Secretary of Transportation has a wide range of delegated responsibilities, including executive management of the nation's transportation resources in periods of crisis. A detailed account of Department of Transportation responsibilities is contained in JP 4-01.

The transportation infrastructure consists of common-user military and commercial assets, services, and systems organic to, contracted for, or controlled by DOD and are commonly referred to as the DTS. Combining the capabilities of common-user transportation assets into an integrated network optimizes the use of available transportation capabilities, provides greater visibility over operations, and eases the transition from peace to war.

Defense Logistics Agency

DLA is a strategic and operational-level logistic agency of the DOD. DLA provides worldwide logistic support to the military departments and the combatant commands across the range of military operations, as well as to other DOD components, federal agencies, foreign governments, or international organizations. DLA provides materiel and supplies to the Services and supports their acquisition of weapons and other equipment. The DLA facilities range from supply centers and depots employing several thousand personnel to in-plant residencies and property disposal offices of fewer than ten people.

Supply and Distribution

DLA buys and manages a vast number and variety of items used by Services and civilian agencies. Commodities include fuel, food, clothing, and medical supplies. In addition, DLA buys and distributes hardware and electronic items used in the maintenance and repair of military equipment. DLA supply centers consolidate the Services' requirements and procure the supplies in sufficient quantities to meet the Services' projected needs. The supplies are stored and distributed through a complex of depots and a single, unified supply distribution system managed by DLA.

Support Services

In addition to supply and distribution, DLA offers the following logistic support services:

- Defense Logistics Information Service manages the Federal Supply Catalog System, which lists national stock numbers and descriptions of over 6 million items.

- Defense National Stockpile Center maintains the defense national stockpile of strategic and critical materials to reduce the nation's dependence upon foreign sources of supply in times of national emergency. The center is authorized to procure and dispose of materials as needed.

- Defense Reutilization and Marketing Service provides for the redistribution and disposal of DOD equipment and supplies no longer needed by the original user. Assets are matched against requirements of the Services and Federal agencies and transferred as needed.

- Document Automated and Production Service is a DLA field command responsible for document automation and printing within DOD.

- Deployed contingency support team (DCST) is deployed by DLA to conduct in-theater operations to support the CINC or JTF staff. DLA may assign a DCST LNO to the MARFOR. The DCST is DLA's in-theater single point of contact to a JFC. Upon request, the DLA deploys an initial response team to determine precise DLA support requirements, then adds functional teams to establish a theater-specific DCST. The DCST serves as the point of contact for numerous items (e.g., fuels support, supply management, reutilization and marketing, contingency contract administration, disaster relief distribution operations management, and disaster relief mobilization center operations).

Marine Corps Strategic Logistics

Strategic logistic support for the MARFOR is provided through the Marine Corps Mobilization Management Plan (MPLAN) and war reserve materiel (WRM).

Marine Corps Mobilization Management Plan

The MPLAN provides service-wide mobilization policy, planning guidance, and responsibilities as part of the CMC's statutory responsibilities. MPLAN assigns mobilization functions and responsibilities to the SE and combatant component commands. Strategic logistic agencies of the Marine Corps SE send detachments and assistance teams into theater to assist the MARFOR staff in coordinating operational-level logistic functions. Primary support is provided through MARCORMATCOM and its subordinate commands, MCLBs and MARCORSYSCOM.

The planning guidance in the MPLAN provides a framework for rapid and efficient mobilization of the personnel and material to meet the Marine Corps wartime requirements. MPLAN Annex B contains a list of significant tasks and responsibilities in the mobilization process; Annex C addresses mobilization logistics. Once the operational decisions are made, the execution of mobilization is largely a manpower and logistic effort, because often a manpower action generates a logistic requirement.

Logistics

Annex C to the MPLAN provides the broad roles and missions necessary to support the mobilization logistic concept of the Marine Corps. The annex provides guidance, procedures, and tasks concerning logistical matters that require action/review during each phase of an operation. Annex C includes required actions for reserve force activation and identifies and describes tasks and responsible section(s) required to provide support. The annex supplements, and must be used in conjunction with, the Marine Corps Capabilities Plan and FDP&E that address deployment support and basic operational logistic support policy and procedures. Roles of subordinate commands remain as stated in the Marine Corps Capabilities Plan, except as amplified in the MPLAN.

The Marine Corps mobilizes its logistic capabilities through expansion of its peacetime support structure to meet wartime requirements. Under the general direction of the CMC and direct coordination authority of force commanders, existing bases and stations are augmented to provide administrative, training, and logistic support to deploying forces, to include units and individuals of the Marine Corps Reserve mobilized to augment the active force structure.

Manpower

Deputy Commandant of the Marine Corps for Plans, Policies, and Operations, HQMC, has staff cognizance over Marine Corps mobilization planning and execution to ensure rapid and efficient expansion of the Marine Corps. In addition, the Deputy Commandant directs Commander, Marine Corps Forces Reserve (COMMARFORRES), to activate SMCR units.

The Marine component commander is responsible for—

- Providing and sustaining forces for the supported CINC.
- Identifying operational unit and Reserve Component individual personnel requirements (to include Navy personnel).
- Identifying SMCR unit activation requirements, including Individual Ready Reserves and individual mobilization augmentees, to CMC.
- Planning for and assimilating Reserve units and personnel into the active operating forces.
- Receiving and resolving Reserve unit equipment shortfalls identified by COMMARFORRES.
- Identifying, collecting, repairing, preserving, and redistributing RBE.
- Maintaining TPFDD.

- Moving SMCR units into theater and returning SMCR equipment at demobilization.
- Consolidating MARFOR requirements.
- Prioritizing assets within specified theaters.
- Coordinating the mobilization, training, deployment, and sustainment of deployed forces and the SE.
- Maintaining the expeditionary logistic nature of MAGTFs.
- Ensuring that the logistic processes do not hamper deployment of MAGTFs and initial reinforcement by the Reserve Component.

Commanders determine the priority and oversee the requisition and application of material to force requirements from all sources. Commander, MCLBs, and Commander, MARCORSYSCOM, provide designated ground materiel to forces and stations. The materiel to support aviation flying units or installations is provided by designated Navy systems commands through fleet type commanders as directed, coordinated, and overseen by commanders for its air forces and/or CMC for Marine Corps installations.

The component commander will plan and coordinate the transportation interface into JOPES. Joint and Service procedures will be used to implement integrated mobilization and deployment support agencies' efforts. Detailed supporting plans must be developed by bases/stations during the deliberate planning process and coordinated with the MARFOR commander. These detailed plans will ensure that materiel is prepared for mobilization, facilities are expanded as necessary, and services are available to support training and subsequent deployment.

War Reserve Materiel

The WRM requirement is the total requirement of supplies and equipment to train, equip, field, and sustain forces in combat based on the requirements of the MEFs, to include assigned SMCR units. The WRM system ensures that materiel assets are available to the operating forces to support combat operations until the DOD materiel distribution system is able to provide support on a sustained basis. In addition, the WRM system is designed to identify the procurement, storage, and preservation of additional materiel requirements used to satisfy increased consumption rates experienced in a combat environment. See MCO P4400.39G, *War Reserve Materiel (WRM) Policy Manual.*

APPENDIX A. NOTIONAL DIVISIONS OF LABOR

The functional responsibilities for operational-level logistics and CSS between the MARFOR, MLC, and MEF/FSSG are described in the notional division of labor tables on the following pages. The task organization and C2 measures necessary for MARFOR success depend on the quantity and variety of tasks, logistic requirements, and time distance factors. The MARFOR, in coordination with its major subordinate commands, will establish the division of labor for the actual contingency or operation. This division of labor could incorporate Service components and supporting activities such as, DLA, MARCORMATCOM, Army TSC, and other joint theater support agencies.

Table A-1. Division of Labor for Supply.

Category	MARFOR	MLC	MEF/FSSG
Class II, III (P), IV, and IX (nonreparables) Supply Support	Sets DIRLAUTH parameters between MLC, supporting activities, and supported units. Monitors component-level issues/trends. Provides coordination of support to Navy forces.	Operates a general account and intermediate supply support activity.	Serves as a material issue point to the MLC general account.
Class I Subsistence	Sets DIRLAUTH parameters between MLC, supporting activities, and supported units. Monitors component-level issues/trends.	Maintains MARFOR theater stocks per OPLAN. (DLA may bypass MLC and throughput Class I to point of consumption defined as the FSSG.)	Provides GS to MEF. Passes back orders to MLC or direct to DLA based on OPLAN.
Class III (B) Bulk POL	Coordinates initial requirements through wartime HNS submission and common item support. Provides a representative to SAPO and monitors component-level issues/trends. Sets DIRLAUTH parameters between MLC, supporting activities, and supported units.	Coordinates POL support with JPO/SAPO. Provides DS to FSSG.	Provides GS to MEF.
Class V(W) Ground Ammunition	Monitors stockage objectives. Coordinates inter-Service transfers with other components to fill shortfalls. Monitors, coordinates, and executes theater-level common item support through major subordinate commands.	Provides DS to the FSSG. Coordinates with DLA and executive agent for Marine Corps requirements.	Provides GS to MEF.
Class V (A) Aviation Ammunition	Consolidates requirements. Sets DIRLAUTH parameters between MLC, supporting activities, and supported units. Monitors component-level issues/trends.	Receives and distributes to ammunition distribution points and ammunition transfer points (likely a coordinator and expediter to avoid double handling).	Stores and issues to Marine aviation logistics squadrons.
Class VIII	Sets DIRLAUTH parameters between MLC and SIMLM. Provides blood usage estimates to JBPO based on intelligence data. Monitors trends and cross-leveling.	Provides DS to FSSG. Coordinates requirements with the SIMLM. (DLA may bypass MLC and control Class VIII to point of consumption defined as the FSSG.)	Provides GS to MEF. Passes back orders to MLC or direct to DLA based on OPLAN.
Class IX Reparables	Sets DIRLAUTH parameters between MLC, supporting activities, and supported units. Coordinates MSC common item support requirements and submits to appropriate theater agency. Monitors Service component-level issues/trends.	Overhauls end items and secondary reparables, evacuates or requests disposition. Coordinates overall availability with MARCORMATCOM.	Conducts 1st through 3d echelon repair. Evacuates to MLC if beyond capability.
Contracting	Passes contracting requirements to MLC. Provides LNO to CLPSB.	Serves as lead contracting agent for MARFOR. Provides representatives to CLPSB, if directed by MARFO.	Submits requirements to MLC. Serves as lead contracting agent for MARFOR, if MLC is not established. Conducts micro purchases within limits of government credit cards.
Salvage/ Disposal	Monitors operations.	Evacuates from force combat service support area (FCSSA) to joint collection point.	Operates MEF collection point at FCSSA.

Table A-2. Division of Labor for Maintenance.

Category	MARFOR	MLC	FSSG
Repair	Establishes minimum reporting requirement. Monitors MSC output reports for trends and readiness indicators.	Provides general support maintenance. Conducts 4th echelon component rebuild. Retrogrades and processes to depots.	Provides DS intermediate 3d echelon maintenance when MLC is established. Provides overflow organization maintenance support and maintenance support teams to MEF units. Assumes GS maintenance role until MLC is established.
Modifications	Monitors MSC output reports for trends and readiness indicators.	Conducts urgent 4th echelon modifications.	Conducts urgent 2d/3d echelon modifications.
Rebuild and Overhaul	Monitors MSC output reports for trends and readiness indicators.	Provides component rebuild and limited 5th echelon depot maintenance when capability is provided in-theater by MARCORMATCOM.	Provides critical component rebuild until MLC is established.
Reclamation	Arranges depot support beyond MARFOR capability.	Retrogrades and processes to depot.	Establishes MEF collection area in FCSSA.
Recovery and Evacuation	Coordinates support external to the MARFOR.	Evacuates from FCSSA.	Provides maintenance support teams and recovery of MEF equipment to collection area in FCSSA.
Inspection and Classification	Monitors MSC output reports for trends and readiness indicators.	Conducts limited technical inspections for follow-on MPF and MEF equipment. Provides overflow support to FSSG.	Conducts limited technical inspections for initial MPF equipment until MLC is established. Conducts limited technical inspection of equipment and identifies level of repair.
Testing	Monitors MSC output reports for trends and readiness indicators.	Repairs test, measurement and diagnostic equipment and conducts 4th echelon testing.	Tests, as appropriate, for organizational and DS 3d echelon maintenance.
Calibration	Monitors MSC output reports for trends and readiness indicators.	Assumes primary responsibility.	Calibrates multimeter and torque meter.

Table A-3. Division of Labor for Transportation.

Category	MARFOR	MLC	FSSG
Port and Terminal Operations, Container Planning, and Intermodal Transportation Management	Monitors operations.	Assumes primary function once established in theater. Assumes responsibility for overall container management and throughput. Operates intermodal and breakbulk distribution centers.	Provides initial capability until MLC is established. Operates MEF distribution and storage centers.
Motor Transport/ Movement Control	Coordinates movement requirements that exceed MARFOR capabilities with theater MCC. Provides a representative to the JTB and JMC. Provides guidance to the Marine MCC.	Provides GS to the MARFOR. Distributes bulk liquids to the FSSG. Provides cross-boundary coordination for MEF movements outside the MEF AO.	Provides GS to the MEF. Provides DS to selected GCE and ACE units. Distributes bulk liquids within the MEF. Operates the LMCC for movements in MEF AO.
Air Delivery	Monitors operations.	Assumes primary responsibility.	Serves as alternate.
Freight/Passenger Transportation	Monitors operations and resolves issues with theater agencies/services, as required.	Assumes primary responsibility.	Serves as alternate.
MHE	Prioritizes distribution of MHE assets.	Provides for assigned ports, airfields, and beaches.	Provides GS to the MEF.
Landing Support	Monitors operations.	Assumes primary responsibility, once established in theater, for the following: • AACG/DACG. • Beach Support.	Provides initial AACG/ DACG and beach support until MLC is established. Provides helicopter support team support to MEF.

Table A-4. Division of Labor for General Engineering.

Category	MARFOR	MLC	FSSG
Horizontal and Vertical Construction	Resources engineering assets for major subordinate commands, especially float bridging. Revises MARFOR major subordinate command engineer support relationships. Resources host-nation civil assets to repair or improve throughput capability. Provides a representative to the JCMEB and JFUB.	Conducts airfield improvements. Conducts LOC road improvement. Supports ACE on expeditionary airfield establishment. Focuses on improving combat support bases and throughput infrastructure.	Conducts expeditionary construction to improve ammunition dumps, fuel farms, etc. Constructs barriers, bunkers, revetments, and other protective structures in support of MEFs. Focuses on improvements to staging and marshalling areas and MEF main supply route development.
Bulk Liquids Storage	Provides a representative to SAPO, and monitors component-level issues/trends.	Receives and stores bulk liquids from joint theater agencies. Receives and stores bulk liquids from MPF and commercial follow-on shipping.	Operates MEF forward storage facilities.
Bridging	Resources external bridging assets for MARFOR major subordinate commands, as required.	Provides engineers to support FSSG.	Controls bridging capability for support to MEF.
Demolition and Obstacle Removal	Resources engineering assets for major subordinate commands.	Provides mobility, countermobility, and survivability operations for assigned ports, airfields, and beaches.	Conducts mobility, countermobility, and survivability operations in support of the MEF.
Engineer Reconnaissance	Monitors component-level issues/trends.	Focuses on ports, airfield, and inland waterways to be used in support of the MARFOR.	Focuses on roads, bridges, and tunnels in support of the MEF.
Explosive Ordnance Disposal	Follows specific OPLAN/OPORD.	Follows specific OPLAN/OPORD.	Follows specific OPLAN/OPORD.

Table A-5. Division of Labor for HSS.

Category	MARFOR	MLC	FSSG
Health Maintenance	Tracks bed/supply status of level II or higher assets in support of MARFOR. Requests augmentation from JFC.	Shares OPLAN/OPORD-specific responsibility.	Shares OPLAN/OPORD-specific responsibility.
Casualty Collection	Monitors operations.	Provides mass casualty overflow support to the MEF.	Assumes primary responsibility.
Casualty Treatment	Provides operational plans and casualty estimates. Consolidates medical situation reports. Provides data to MLC.	Provides support level III, fleet hospital, if assigned, to the MARFOR during MPF operations.	Provides level I and II support to the MEF.
Temporary Casualty Holding	Monitors operations.	Provides mass casualty overflow support to the MEF.	Assumes primary responsibility.
Casualty Evacuation and Medical Regulating	Tracks status of level II or higher MARFOR patients.	Provides medical regulating for the MARFOR.	Evacuates casualties to MEF level II facility or CRTS.

Table A-6. Division of Labor for Services.

Category	MARFOR	MLC	FSSG
Postal Support	Resolves theater-level issues.	Operates MARFOR post office and forwards mail to FSSG central post office.	Operates central post office and forwards mail to MEF postal detachments. Assumes responsibility for receipt, distribution, dispatch, and financial services to the MEF.
Disbursing Support	Monitors operations.	Operates combined MARFOR disbursing office at MLC.	Operates satellite disbursing offices and Marine pay teams.
Mortuary Affairs	Designates service component mortuary affairs officer. Provides LNO to JMAO.	Processes evacuees to theater agent per JMAO procedures. Coordinates throughput of remains to theater mortuary evacuation point.	Evacuates to MLC mortuary affairs collection point.
Legal Support	Coordinates and directs forces. Resolves theater-level issues. Researches claims procedures.	Operates the consolidated claims office.	Provides legal services to the MEF.
Exchange Services	Resolves theater-level issues.	Assumes primary responsibility. Coordinates with Army and Air Force Exchange Service for common support, as appropriate.	Serves as alternate. Provides mobile tactical field exchange service.

Appendix B. Glossary

Section I. Acronyms and Abbreviations

AAA . . . . arrival and assembly area
AACG . . . . arrival airfield control group
AAOE . . arrival and assembly operations element
AAOG . . . arrival and assembly operations group
ABFC . . . . advanced base functional component
ACE . . . . aviation combat element
ACM . . . . air contingency MAGTF
AC/S . . . . .assistant chief of staff
ACSA . . . . . acquisition cross-Service agreement
A/DACG . . . . arrival/departure airfield
control group
ADCON . . . . administrative control
AE . . . . aeromedical evacuation
AECC . . . . aeromedical evacuation
coordination center
AFCSS . Air Force contingency supply squadron
AIT . . . . . . automated identification technology
ALSS . . . . advanced logistic support site
AMC . . . . Air Mobility Command
AO . . . . .area of operations
AOC . . . . .air operations center
AOR . . . . area of responsibility
APOD . . . . .aerial port of debarkation
APOE . . . . aerial port of embarkation
ARFOR . . . . Army forces
ASBPO . . Armed Services Blood Program Office
ASCC . . . . Army Service Component Command
ASG . . . . area support group
AT . . . . .antiterrorism
ATLASS . . . . Asset Tracking Logistics
and Supply System

BIC . . . . Blount Island Command
bn . . . . battalion
BOG . . . . beach operations group
BSSG . . . . brigade service support group

C2 . . . . .command and control
C4 . . . . command, control, communications,
and computers
CAPS II . . . . . Consolidated Aerial Port System II
CAT . . . . crisis action team
CCIR . . . . commander's critical information
requirements
CE . . . . command element

CEE . . . . captured enemy equipment;
combat essential equipment
CINC . . . . commander in chief
CIS . . .communications and information systems
CJCS . . . . . Chairman of the Joint Chiefs of Staff
CJCSM . . . . Chairman of the Joint Chiefs
of Staff Manual
CLF . . . . combat logistics force
CLPSB . . . . CINC logistic procurement
support board
CMC . . . . .Commandant of the Marine Corps
CNO . . . . Chief of Naval Operations
COA . . . . course of action
COCOM . . . . combatant command
(command authority)
COE . . . . common operating environment
COMAFFOR . . . . .commander, Air Force forces
COMARFOR . . . . .commander, Army forces
COMMARFOR . . . . commander,
Marine Corps forces
COMMARFOREUR . . . . .Commander,
Marine Corps Forces, Europe
COMMARFORLANT . . . . .Commander,
Marine Corps Forces, Atlantic
COMMARFORPAC . . . . .Commander,
Marine Corps Forces, Pacific
COMMARFORRES . . . . .Commander,
Marine Corps Forces Reserve
COMMZ . . . . .communications zone
CONUS . . . . continental United States
COP . . . . common operational picture
COSCOM . . . . .corps support command
CRAF . . . . .civil reserve air fleet
CRTS . . . . casualty receiving and treatment ship
CSB . . . . .corps support battalion
CSE . . . . .client server environment
CSG . . . . corps support group
CSS . . . . combat service support
CSSA . . . . .combat service support area
CSSD . . . . . .combat service support detachment
CSSE . . . . .combat service support element
CSSG . . . . combat service support group
CUL . . . . .common-user logistics

DACG . . . . .departure airfield control group

DAL . . . . directive authority for logistics
DCST . . . . . .deployed contingency support team
DESC . . . . defense energy support center
det . . . . .detachment
DIA . . . . .Defense Intelligence Agency
DII . . . . .defense information infrastructure
DIRLAUTH . . . . .direct liaison authorized
DIRMOBFOR. . . . . . . director of mobility forces
DLA . . . . Defense Logistics Agency
DMC . . . . .distribution management center
DOD . . . . Department of Defense
DOMS. . . . . director of military support
DRB . . . . division ready brigade
DS . . . . direct support
DSO . . . . domestic support operations
DTS. . . . . .Defense Transportation System

EAC . . . . .echelons above corps
EMW. . . . . expeditionary maneuver warfare
EPW . . . . enemy prisoner of war
ESB. . . . . engineer support battalion

FALD . . . . field and logistics division
(United Nations)
FBI . . . . .Federal Bureau of Investigation
FCSSA . . . . . . force combat service support area
FDP&E . . . . force deployment
planning and execution
FEMA . . . . Federal Emergency
Management Agency
FLS . . . . forward logistic site
FM. . . . . field manual (Army)
FMCC . . . . force movement control center
FSB . . . . .forward support battalion
FSSG. . . . . force service support group

G-1 . . . . Army or Marine Corps component
manpower or personnel staff
officer/organization
G-2 . . . . Army or Marine Corps component
intelligence staff officer/organization
G-3 . . . . Army or Marine Corps component
operations staff officer/organization
G-4 . . . . Army or Marine Corps component
logistics staff officer/organization
G-5 . . . . plans officer/organization
G-6 . . . . communications and information
systems officer
GCCS . . . Global Command and Control System
GCE . . . . ground combat element

GCSS . . . . .Global Combat Support System
GIRH. . . . . . . Generic Intelligence Requirements
Handbook
GPMRC . . . . Global Patient Movement
Requirements Center
GS . . . . .general support
GSG . . . . general support group
GTN . . . . Global Transportation Network

HHQ . . . . higher headquarters
HNS . . . . .host-nation support
HQMC . . . . Headquarters, Marine Corps
H&S Bn. . . . . .headquarters and service battalion
HSS . . . . health service support
HSV . . . . .high-speed surface vehicle

I&L . . . . installations and logistics
IPB . . .intelligence preparation of the battlespace
IR . . . . .intelligence requirement
ITV . . . . in-transit visibility

J-3 . . . . operations directorate of a joint staff
J-4 . . . . .logistics directorate of a joint staff
J-5 . . . . plans directorate of a joint staff
JBPO. . . . . .Joint Blood Program Office
JCMEB . . . joint civil-military engineering board
JCS . . . . .Joint Chiefs of Staff
JDST . . . . joint decision support tool
JFC . . . . .joint force commander
JFS . . . . .joint force surgeon
JFUB. . . . . Joint Facilities Utilization Board
JIDC . . . joint interrogation and debriefing center
JLOTS. . . . . joint logistics over-the-shore
JMAO . . . . .joint mortuary affairs office
JMC. . . . . joint movement center
JOA. . . . . .joint operations area
JOPES. . . . . Joint Operation Planning
and Execution System
JP. . . . . .joint publication
JPMRC . . . . joint patient movement
requirements center
JPO . . . . .Joint Petroleum Office
JRSOI . . . . joint reception, staging,
onward movement, and integration
JTAV. . . . . joint total asset visibility
JTB . . . . Joint Transportation Board
JTF . . . . .joint task force

LFSP . . . . landing force support party
LMCC . . . . . . .logistic movement control center

LNO . . . . liaison officer
LOC . . . . line of communications
LOGAIS . . . . .logistics automated
information system
LOTS . . . . logistics over-the-shore
LRC. . . . . logistics readiness center
LSB . . . . landing support battalion
LSE . . . . logistics support element
LTF . . . . logistics task force

MACDIS. . . . . military assistance for
civil disturbances
MAG. . . . . .Marine aircraft group
MAGTF . . . . Marine air-ground task force
MAGTF II. . . . . . . Marine air-ground task force
system II
maint . . . . maintenance
MALS . . . . . Marine aviation logistics squadron
MARCORMATCOM. . . . . Marine Corps
Materiel Command
MARCORSYSCOM. . . . . Marine Corps
Systems Command
MARFOR . . . . .Marine Corps forces
MAW . . . . Marine aircraft wing
MCA . . . . movement control agency
MCC . . . . movement control center
MCLB. . . . . .Marine Corps logistics base
MCO . . . . Marine Corps order
MCPP . . . . .Marine Corps Planning Process
MCSSD. . . . . mobile combat service
support detachment
MCWP . . .Marine Corps warfighting publication
MDSS II . . . . .MAGTF Deployment
Support System II
MEB . . . . Marine expeditionary brigade
med . . . . .medical
MEDCC . . . . .medical coordination center
MEF . . . . Marine expeditionary force
METT-T . . .mission, enemy, terrain and weather,
troops and support
available-time available
MEU . . . . Marine expeditionary unit
MHE . . . . materials handling equipment
MILU . . . . .multinational integrated logistic unit
MIMMS . . . . . . .Marine Integrated Maintenance
Management System
MJLC . . . . multinational joint logistic center
MLC . . . . .Marine Logistics Command

MNF .multinational force
MNFC. . . . . . . .multinational force commander
MNL . . . . multinational logistics
MNLC. . . . . .multinational logistic center
MOOTW. . . . . military operations other than war
MPE/S. . . . . . maritime pre-positioned equipment
and supplies
MPF . . . . maritime pre-positioning force
MPF(F) . . . . MPF (Future)
MPLAN . . . . Marine Corps Mobilization
Management Plan
MPS . . . . maritime pre-positioning ship
MPSRON . . . . maritime pre-positioning
ships squadron
MSC . . . . Military Sealift Command
MSCA. . . . . . military support to civil authorities
MSCLEA . . . . . . military support to civilian law
enforcement agencies
MSSG . . . . . . Marine expeditionary unit (MEU)
service support group
MT Bn. . . . . motor transport battalion
MTF . . . . medical treatment facility
MTMC . . . . Military Traffic
Management Command
MTW. . . . . major theater war
MWSG . . . . Marine wing support group
MWSS. . . . . Marine wing support squadron

NALCOMIS . . . . Naval Aviation Logistics
Command Management
Information System
NALMEB . . . . .Norway air-landed Marine
expeditionary brigade
NATO . . . . . . North Atlantic Treaty Organization
NAVAIRSYSCOM . . . . Naval Air
Systems Command
NAVFACENGCOM. . . . . naval facilities
engineering command
NCA . . . . National Command Authorities
NCC . . . . Navy component command
NCF. . . . . .naval construction force
NGO . . . . .nongovernmental organization
NMCB. . . . . .naval mobile construction battalion
NSE. . . . . national support element
NWP . . . . .naval warfare publication

OCONUS . .outside the continental United States
OPCON. . . . . operational control

OPLAN . . . . .operation plan
OPORD .operation order
OPREP . . . . .operational report
OPT . . . . operational planning team

PDE&A . . . . planning, decision, execution,
and assessment
PKO . . . . peacekeeping operations
POG . . . . .port operations group
POL . . . . .petroleum, oils, and lubricants

RBE . . . . remain-behind equipment
rein . . . . reinforcing
RIK . . . . .replacement-in-kind
RRF . . . . Ready Reserve Force
RSOI . . . . reception, staging, onward
movement, and integration

SAPO . . . . subarea petroleum office
SASSY . . . . .supported activities supply systems
SE . . . . supporting establishment
SEABEE . . . . Navy construction engineer
SECDEF . . . . Secretary of Defense
SIMLM . . . . single integrated medical
logistics manager
SITREP .situation report
SMCR . . . . .Selected Marine Corps Reserve
SNAP III . . . . .Shipboard Nontactical Automated
Data Processing Program III
SPMAGTF . . . . special purpose Marine
air-ground task force
SPOD . . . . seaport of debarkation
SPOE . . . . .seaport of embarkation

T/E . . . . table of equipment
TAA . . . . .tactical assembly area
TAAT . . . . . . .technical assistance advisory team
T-AVB . . . . aviation logistics support ship
TC-AIMS . . . . Transportation Coordinator's
Automated Information for
Movement System
TCC . . . . . . transportation component command
TMCC . . . .theater movement coordination center
TPFDD . . . . .time-phased force
and deployment data
TPMRC . . . . .theater patient movement
requirements center
TSC . . . . .theater support command

UMCC . . . . unit movement control center
UNAAF . . . . Unified Action Armed Forces
USAMC . . . . United States Army
Materiel Command
USCINCTRANS . . . . .Commander in Chief,
United States Transportation
Command
USJFCOM . . . . United States
Joint Forces Command
USPACOM . . . . United States Pacific Command
USSOCOM . . . . United States Special
Operations Command
USSOUTHCOM . . . . .United States Southern
Command
USTRANSCOM . . . United States Transportation
Command

WRMSF . . . . . . war reserve materiel stocks field

SECTION II. DEFINITIONS

advanced base—A base located in or near a theater of operations whose primary mission is to support military operations. (JP 1-02)

allocation—In a general sense, distribution of limited resources among competing requirements for employment. Specific allocations (e.g., air sorties, nuclear weapons, forces, and transportation) are described as allocation of air sorties, nuclear weapons, etc. (JP-1-02)

apportionment—In the general sense, distribution for planning of limited resources among competing requirements. Specific apportionments (e.g., air sorties and forces for planning) are described as apportionment of air sorties and forces for planning, etc. (JP-1-02)

area of responsibility—The geographical area associated with a combatant command within which a combatant commander has authority to plan and conduct operations. (JP 1-02)

assign—1. To place units or personnel in an organization where such placement is relatively permanent, and/or where such organization controls and administers the units or personnel for the primary function, or greater portion of the functions, of the unit or personnel. 2. To detail individuals to specific duties or functions where such duties or functions are primary and/ or relatively permanent. (JP-1-02)

base—1. A locality from which operations are projected or supported. 2. An area or locality containing installations which provide logistic or other support. 3. Home airfield or home carrier. (JP 1-02)

branch(es)—A contingency plan or course of action (an option built into the basic plan or course of action) for changing the mission, disposition, orientation, or direction of movement of the force to aid success of the operation based on anticipated events, opportunities, or disruptions caused by enemy actions. (MCRP 5-12C)

campaign—A series of related military operations aimed at accomplishing a strategic or operational objective within a given time and space. (JP 1-02)

campaign plan—A plan for a series of related military operations aimed at accomplishing a strategic or operational objective within a given time and space. (JP 1-02)

campaign planning—The process whereby combatant commanders and subordinate joint force commanders translate national or theater strategy into operational concepts through the development of campaign plans. Campaign planning may begin during deliberate planning when the actual threat, national guidance, and available resources become evident, but is normally not completed until after the National Command Authorities select the course of action during crisis action planning. Campaign planning is conducted when contemplated military operations exceed the scope of a single major joint operation. (JP 1-02)

centers of gravity—Those characteristics, capabilities, or localities from which a military force derives its freedom of action, physical strength, or will to fight. (JP 1-02)

combatant command—A unified or specified command with a broad continuing mission under a single commander established and so designated by the President, through the Secretary of Defense and with the advice and assistance of the Chairman of the Joint Chiefs of Staff. Combatant commands typically have geographic or functional responsibilities. (JP 1-02)

combatant command (command authority)—Nontransferable command authority established by title 10 ("Armed Forces"), United States Code, section 164, exercised only by commanders of unified or specified combatant commands unless otherwise directed by the President or the Secretary of Defense. Combatant command (command authority) cannot be delegated and is the authority of a combatant commander to perform those functions of command over assigned forces involving organizing and employing commands and forces, assigning tasks, designating objectives, and giving authoritative direction over all aspects of military operations, joint training, and logistics necessary to accomplish the missions assigned to the command. Combatant command (command authority) should be exercised through the commanders of subordinate organizations. Normally this authority is exercised through subordinate joint force commanders and Service and/or functional component commanders. Combatant command (command authority) provides full authority to organize and employ commands and forces as the combatant commander considers necessary to accomplish assigned missions. Operational control is inherent in combatant command (command authority). Also called **COCOM**. (JP 1-02)

combatant commander—A commander in chief of one of the unified or specified combatant commands established by the President. Also called **CINC**. (JP 1-02)

commander's critical information requirements—A comprehensive list of information requirements identified by the commander as being critical in facilitating timely information management and the decisionmaking process that affect successful mission accomplishment. The two key subcomponents are critical friendly force information and priority intelligence requirements. Also called **CCIR**. (JP 1-02)

common item—Any item of materiel that is required for use by more than one activity. Items used by two or more Military Services of similar manufacture or fabrication that may vary between the Services as to color or shape (as vehicles or clothing). (extract from JP 1-02)

common servicing—That function performed by one Military Service in support of another Military Service for which reimbursement is not required from the Service receiving support. (JP 1-02)

common use—Services, materials, or facilities provided by a Department of Defense agency or a Military Department on a common basis for two or more Department of Defense agencies. (based on JP 1-02)

common-user logistics—Materiel, items, or service support shared with or provided by two or more Services, Department of Defense (DOD) agencies, or multinational partners to another Service, DOD agency, non-DOD agency, and/or multinational partner in an operation. Common-user logistics is usually restricted to a particular type of supply and/or service and may be further restricted to specific unit(s) or types of units, specific times, missions, and/or geographic areas. Also called **CUL**. (Proposed for JP 1-02 by JP 4-07)

communications zone—Rear part of a theater of operations (behind but contiguous to the combat zone) which contains the lines of communications, establishments for supply and evacuation, and other agencies required for the immediate support and maintenance of the field forces. (JP 1-02)

contingency—An emergency involving military forces caused by natural disasters, terrorists, subversives, or by required military operations. Due to the uncertainty of the situation, contingencies require plans, rapid response, and special procedures to ensure the safety and readiness of personnel, installations, and equipment. (JP 1-02)

course of action—**1.** A plan that would accomplish, or is related to, the accomplishment of a mission. **2.** The scheme adopted to accomplish a task or mission. It is a product of the Joint Operation Planning and Execution System concept development phase. The supported commander will include a recommended course of action in the commander's estimate. The recommended course of action will include the concept of operations, evaluation of supportability estimates of supporting organizations, and an integrated time-phased data base of combat, combat support, and combat service support forces and sustainment. Refinement of this database will be contingent on the time available for course of action development. When approved, the course of action becomes the basis for the development of an operation plan or operation order. Also called **COA**. (JP 1-02)

crisis action planning—1. The Joint Operation Planning and Execution System process involving the time-sensitive development of joint operation plans and orders in response to an imminent crisis. Crisis action planning follows prescribed crisis action procedures to formulate and implement an effective response within the time frame permitted by the crisis. 2. The time-sensitive planning for the deployment, employment, and sustainment of assigned and allocated forces and resources that occurs in response to a situation that may result in actual military operations. Crisis action planners base their plan on the circumstances that exist at the time planning occurs. Also called **CAP**. (JP 1-02)

cross-servicing—That function performed by one Military Service in support of another Military Service for which reimbursement is required from the Service receiving support. (JP 1-02)

Defense Communications System—Department of Defense long-haul voice, data, and record traffic system which includes the Defense Data Network, Defense Satellite Communications System, and Defense Switched Network. Also called **DCS**. (JP 1-02)

Defense Information Systems Network—Integrated network, centrally managed and configured to provide long-haul information transfer services for all Department of Defense activities. It is an information transfer utility designed to provide dedicated point-to-point, switched voice and data, imagery, and video teleconferencing services. Also called **DISN**. (JP 1-02)

deliberate planning—1. The Joint Operation Planning and Execution System process involving the development of joint operation plans for contingencies identified in joint strategic planning documents. Conducted principally in peacetime, deliberate planning is accomplished in prescribed cycles that complement other Department of Defense planning cycles in accordance with the formally established Joint Strategic Planning System. 2. A planning process for the deployment and employment of apportioned forces and resources that occurs in response to a hypothetical situation. Deliberate planners rely heavily on assumptions regarding the circumstances that will exist when the plan is executed. (JP 1-02)

deployment—1. In naval usage, the change from a cruising approach or contact disposition to a disposition for battle. 2. The movement of forces within areas of operation. 3. The positioning of forces into a formation for battle. 4. The relocation of forces and materiel to desired areas of operations. Deployment encompasses all activities from origin or home station through destination, specifically including intra-continental United States, intertheater, and intratheater movement legs, staging, and holding areas. (JP 1-02)

deployment planning—Operational planning directed toward the movement of forces and sustainment resources from their original locations to a specific operational area for conducting the joint operations contemplated in a given plan. Encompasses all activities from origin or home station through destination, specifically including intra-continental United States, intertheater, and intratheater movement legs, staging areas, and holding areas. (JP 1-02)

directive authority for logistics—Combatant commander authority to issue directives to subordinate commanders, including peacetime measures, necessary to ensure the effective execution of approved operation plans. Essential measures include the optimized use or reallocation of available resources and prevention or elimination of redundant facilities and/or overlapping functions among the Service component commands. (Proposed for JP 1-02 by JP 0-2)

displaced person—A civilian who is involuntarily outside the national boundaries of his or her country. (JP 1-02)

dominant user concept—The concept that the Service which is the principal consumer will have the responsibility for performance of a support workload for all using Services. (JP 1-02)

employment—The strategic, operational, or tactical use of forces. (JP 1-02)

employment planning—Planning that prescribes how to apply force/forces to attain specified military objectives. Employment planning concepts are developed by combatant commanders through their component commanders. (JP 1-02)

evacuee—A civilian removed from a place of residence by military direction for reasons of personal security or the requirements of the military situation. (JP 1-02)

execution planning—The phase of the Joint Operation Planning and Execution System crisis action planning process that provides for the translation of an approved course of action into an executable plan of action through the preparation of a complete operation plan or operation order. Execution planning is detailed planning for the commitment of specified forces and resources. During crisis action planning, an approved operation plan or other National Command Authorities-approved course of action is adjusted, refined, and translated into an operation order. Execution planning can proceed on the basis of prior deliberate planning, or it can take place in the absence of prior planning. (JP 1-02)

executive agent—A term used in Department of Defense and Service regulations to indicate a delegation of authority by a superior to a subordinate to act on behalf of the superior. An agreement between equals does not create an executive agent. For example, a Service cannot become a Department of Defense executive agent for a particular matter with simply the agreement of the other Services; such authority must be delegated by the Secretary of Defense. Designation as executive agent, in and of itself, confers no authority. The exact nature and scope of the authority delegated must be stated in the document designating the executive agent. An executive agent may be limited to providing only administration and support or coordinating common functions, or it may be delegated authority, direction, and control over specified resources for specified purposes. (JP 1-02)

force deployment planning and execution—Operational procedures during deliberate or crises action planning, and the execution of those plans, to support the maneuver of forces and sustainment within the battlespace based on a concept of employment.

force module—A grouping of combat, combat support, and combat service support forces, with their accompanying supplies and the required non-unit resupply and personnel necessary to sustain forces for a minimum of 30 days. The elements of force modules are linked together or are uniquely identified so that they may be extracted from or adjusted as an entity in the Joint Operation Planning and Execution System data bases to enhance flexibility and usefulness of the operation plan during a crisis. Also called **FM**. (JP 1- 02)

functional plans—Plans involving the conduct of military operations in a peacetime or permissive environment developed by combatant commanders to address requirements such as disaster relief, nation assistance, logistics, communications, surveillance, protection of US citizens, nuclear weapon recovery and evacuation, and continuity of operations, or similar discrete tasks. They may be developed in response to the requirements of the Joint Strategic Capabilities Plan, at the initiative of the CINC, or as tasked by the supported combatant commander, Joint Staff, Service, or Defense agency. Chairman of the

Joint Chiefs of Staff review of CINC-initiated plans is not normally required. (JP 1-02)

Global Command and Control System—Highly mobile, deployable command and control system supporting forces for joint and multinational operations across the range of military operations, any time and anywhere in the world with compatible, interoperable, and integrated command, control, communications, computers, and intelligence systems. Also called **GCCS**. (JP 1-02)

global transportation network—The automated support necessary to enable USTRANSCOM and its components to provide global transportation management. The global transportation network provides the integrated transportation data and systems necessary to accomplish global transportation planning, command and control, and in-transit visibility across the range of military operations. Also called **GTN**. (JP 1-02)

implementation planning—Operational planning associated with the conduct of a continuing operation, campaign, or war to attain defined objectives. At the national level, it includes the development of strategy and the assignment of strategic tasks to the combatant commanders. At the theater level, it includes the development of campaign plans to attain assigned objectives and the preparation of operation plans and operation orders to prosecute the campaign. At lower levels, implementation planning prepares for the execution of assigned tasks or logistic missions. (JP 1-02)

integrated material manager—Any activity/agency designated to exercise integrated material management for a Federal supply group/class commodity or item on a DOD or Federal Government level. (User Manual 4400.71)

integration—In force projection, the synchronized transfer of units into an operational commander's force prior to mission execution. (JP 1-02)

intelligence requirement—**1.** Any subject, general or specific, upon which there is a need for the collection of information or the production of intelligence. (JP 1-02) **2.** In Marine Corps usage, questions about the enemy and the environment, the answers to which a commander requires to make sound decisions. Also called **IR**. (MCRP 5-12C)

international logistic support—The provision of military logistic support by one participating nation to one or more participating nations, either with or without reimbursement. (JP 1-02)

interagency coordination—Within the context of Department of Defense involvement, the coordination that occurs between elements of the Department of Defense and engaged US Government agencies, nongovernmental organizations, private voluntary organizations, and regional and international organizations for the purpose of accomplishing an objective. (JP 1-02)

internally displaced person—Any person who has left his habitual residence due to fear of persecution or natural disaster but has not left his own country.

inter-Service support—Action by one Military Service or element thereof to provide logistic and/or administrative support to another Military Service or element thereof. Such action can be recurring or nonrecurring in character on an installation, area, or worldwide basis. (JP 1-02)

joint force—A general term applied to a force composed of significant elements, assigned or attached, of two or more Military Departments, operating under a single joint force commander. (JP 0-1)

joint force commander—A general term applied to a combatant commander, subunified commander, or joint task force commander authorized to exercise combatant command (command authority) or operational control over a joint force. Also called **JFC**. See also **joint force**. (JP 1-02)

joint logistics—The art and science of planning and carrying out, by a joint force commander and staff, logistic operations to support the protection, movement, maneuver, firepower, and sustainment of operating forces of two or more Military Departments of the same nation. (JP 1-02)

Joint Mobility Control Group—The Joint Mobility Control Group is the focal point for coordinating and optimizing transportation operations. This group is comprised of seven essential elements. The primary elements are USTRANSCOM's Mobility Control Center (MCC), Joint Operational Support Airlift Center (JOSAC), Global Patient Movement Requirements Center (GPMRC), Tanker Airlift Control Center (TACC), Military Sealift Command Command Center, Military Traffic Management Command Command Operations and the Joint Intelligence Center-USTRANSCOM (JIC-TRANS). Also called **JMCG**. (JP 1-02)

joint mortuary affairs office—Plans and executes all mortuary affairs programs within a theater. Provides guidance to facilitate the conduct of all mortuary programs and to maintain data (as required) pertaining to recovery, identification, and disposition of all US dead and missing in the assigned theater. Serves as the central clearing point for all mortuary affairs and monitors the deceased and missing personal effects program. Also called **JMAO**. (JP 1-02)

joint movement center—The center established to coordinate the employment of all means of transportation (including that provided by allies or host nations) to support the concept of operations. This coordination is accomplished through establishment of transportation policies within the assigned operational area, consistent with relative urgency of need, port and terminal capabilities, transportation asset availability, and priorities set by a joint force commander. (JP 1-02)

joint operations area—An area of land, sea, and airspace, defined by a geographic combatant commander or subordinate unified commander, in which a joint force commander (normally a joint task force commander) conducts military operations to accomplish a specific mission. Joint operations areas are particularly useful when operations are limited in scope and geographic area or when operations are to be conducted on the boundaries between theaters. Also called **JOA**. (JP 1-02)

joint operations center—A jointly manned facility of a joint force commander's headquarters established for planning, monitoring, and guiding the execution of the commander's decisions. Also called **JOC**. (JP 1-02)

joint planning and execution community—Those headquarters, commands, and agencies involved in the training, preparation, movement, reception, employment, support, and sustainment of military forces assigned or committed to a theater of operations or objective area. It usually consists of the Joint Staff, Services, Service major commands (including the Service wholesale logistic commands), unified commands (and their certain Service component commands), sub-unified commands, transportation component commands, joint task forces (as applicable), Defense Logistics Agency, and other Defense agencies (e.g., Defense Intelligence Agency) as may be appropriate to a given scenario. Also called **JPEC**. (JP 1-02)

joint rear area—A specific land area within a joint force commander's operational area designated to facilitate protection and operation of installations and forces supporting the joint force. Also called **JRA**. (JP 1-02)

joint rear area coordinator—The officer with responsibility for coordinating the overall security of the joint rear area in accordance with joint force commander directives and priorities in order to assist in providing a secure environment to facilitate sustainment, host nation support, infrastructure development, and movements of the joint force. The joint rear area coordinator also coordinates intelligence support and ensures that area management is practiced with due consideration for security requirements. (JP 1-02)

joint rear area operations—Those operations in the joint rear area that facilitate protection or support of the joint force. (JP 1-02)

joint rear tactical operations center—A joint operations cell tailored to assist the joint rear area coordinator in meeting mission responsibilities. (JP 1-02)

joint reception, staging, onward movement, and integration—A phase of joint force projection occurring in the operational area. This phase comprises the essential processes required to transition arriving personnel, equipment, and materiel into forces capable of meeting operational requirements. Also called **JRSO&I**. (JP 1-02)

joint servicing—That function performed by a jointly staffed and financed activity in support of two or more Military Services. (JP 1-02)

joint task force—A joint force that is constituted and so designated by the Secretary of Defense, a combatant commander, a subunified commander, or an existing joint task force commander. Also called **JTF**. (JP 1-02)

lead agent—Individual Services, combatant commands, or Joint Staff directorates may be assigned as lead agents for developing and maintaining joint doctrine, joint tactics, techniques, and procedures (JTTP) publications. The lead agent is responsible for developing, coordinating, reviewing, and maintaining an assigned doctrine or JTTP. (JP 1-02)

lead nation—A nation that has agreed to assume responsibility for procuring or providing logistics to all or part of the multinational force within a designated geographic region.

level of supply—The quantity of supplies or materiel authorized or directed to be held in anticipation of future demands. (JP 1-02)

liaison—That contact or intercommunication maintained between elements of military forces or other agencies to ensure mutual understanding and unity of purpose and action. (JP 1-02)

line of communications—A route of either land, water, and/or air, that connects an operating military force with a base of operations and along which supplies and military forces move. Also called **LOC**. (JP 1-02)

Marine Logistic Operations Center—The MLC command and control center modeled after the FSSG-level combat service support operations center (CSSOC). Also called **MLOC**.

migrant—A person who left home temporarily or permanently for economic reasons. (Webster)

most capable Service or agency—The organization that is best suited to provide common supply commodity or logistic service support within a specific joint operation. In this context, "best suited" could mean the Service or agency that has required or readily available resources and/or expertise. The most capable Service may or may not be the dominant user in any particular operation. (Proposed for JP 1-02 by JP 4-07)

movement control—**1.** The planning, routing, scheduling, and control of personnel and cargo movements over lines of communications. **2.** An organization responsible for the planning, routing, scheduling, and control of personnel and cargo movements over lines of communications. Also called **movement control center**. (JP 1-02)

multinational integrated logistic support—Two or more nations agree to provide logistic assets to a multinational logistics force under the operational control of a multinational force commander. These assets will be used for the logistic support of the entire force.

multinational logistic support agreement—Any arrangement involving two or more countries that aims at the logistic support of a force (either the forces of the countries participating in the arrangement or other countries).

mutual support arrangements—Any formal agreement signed between or among nations, which documents the scope, terms, and conditions of a multinational logistic support arrangement. It includes, but is not limited to, U.S. acquisition and cross-servicing agreements, NATO mutual support agreements, host-nation support agreements, etc.

onward movement—The relocation of forces capable of meeting the commander's operational requirements to the initial point of their mission execution. This includes the movement of associated sustainment, personnel, equipment and materiel.

operation order—A directive issued by a commander to subordinate commanders for the purpose of effecting the coordinated execution of an operation. Also called **OPORD**. (JP 1-02)

operation plan—Any plan, except for the Single Integrated Operational Plan, for the conduct of military operations. Plans are prepared by combatant commanders in response to requirements established by the Chairman of the Joint Chiefs of Staff and by commanders of subordinate commands in response to requirements tasked by the establishing unified commander. Operation plans are prepared in either a complete format (OPLAN) or as a concept plan (CONPLAN). The CONPLAN can be published with or without a time-phased force and deployment data (TPFDD) file. **a. OPLAN**. An operation plan for the conduct of joint operations that can be used as a basis for development of an operation order (OPORD). An OPLAN identifies the forces and supplies required to execute the CINC's Strategic Concept and a movement schedule of these resources to the theater of operations. The forces and supplies are identified in TPFDD files. OPLANs will include all phases of the tasked operation. The plan is prepared with the appropriate annexes, appendixes, and TPFDD files as described in the Joint Operation Planning and Execution System manuals containing planning policies, procedures, and formats. Also called **OPLAN**. **b. CONPLAN**. An operation plan in an abbreviated format that would require considerable expansion or alteration to convert it into an OPLAN or OPORD. A CONPLAN contains the CINC's Strategic Concept and those annexes and appendixes deemed necessary by the combatant commander to complete planning. Generally, detailed support requirements are not calculated and TPFDD files are not prepared. **c. CONPLAN with TPFDD**. A CONPLAN with TPFDD is the same as a CONPLAN except that it requires more detailed planning for phased deployment of forces. Also called **CONPLAN**. (JP 1-02)

priority intelligence requirements—**1.** Those intelligence requirements for which a commander has an anticipated and stated priority in the task of planning and decisionmaking. (JP 1-02) **2.** In Marine Corps usage, an intelligence requirement associated with a decision that will critically affect the overall success of the command's mission. Also called **PIR**. (MCRP 5-12C)

reception—The process of receiving, offloading, marshalling, and transporting of personnel, equipment, and materiel from the strategic and/or intratheater deployment phase to a sea, air, or surface transportation point of debarkation to the marshalling area. (JP 1-02)

reconstitution—Those actions that commanders plan and implement to restore units to a desired level of combat effectiveness commensurate with mission requirements and available resources. It transcends normal day-to-day force sustainment actions. However, it uses existing systems and units to do so. No resources exist solely to perform reconstitution.

recovery and reconstitution—**1.** Those actions taken by one nation prior to, during, and following an attack by an enemy nation to minimize the effects of the attack, rehabilitate the national economy, provide for the welfare of the populace, and maximize the combat potential of remaining forces and supporting activities. **2.** Those actions taken by a military force during or after operational employment to restore its combat capability to full operational readiness. (JP 1-02)

redeployment—The transfer of forces and materiel to support another joint force commander's operational requirements, or to return personnel, equipment, and materiel to the home and/or demobilization stations for reintegration and/or out-processing. (JP 1-02)

refugee—A civilian who, by reason of real or imagined danger, has left home to seek safety elsewhere. (JP 1-02)

regeneration—One of the two types of reconstitution, it is the rebuilding of a unit to full mission capability. It requires large-scale replacement of personnel, equipment, and supplies. These replacements may then require further reorganization. This is a higher level of reorganization than the unit can do during normal reorganization without adequate personnel resources. Because of the intensive nature of regeneration, it occurs at a regeneration site after the unit disengages. It also requires help from higher echelons and the supporting establishment if conducted in theater.

seavan—Military container moved via ocean. (JP 1-02)

sequel(s)—Major operations that follow the current major operation. Plans for these are based on the possible outcomes (success, stalemate, or defeat) associated with the current operation. (MCRP 5-12C)

Service component command—A command consisting of the Service component commander and all those Service forces, such as individuals, units, detachments, organizations, and installations under that command, including the support forces that have been assigned to a combatant command, or further assigned to a subordinate unified command or joint task force. (JP 1-02)

single port manager—Through its transporation component commands, US Transportation Command is the Department of Defense-designated single port manager for all common-user aerial and sea ports worldwide. The single port manager performs those functions necessary to support the strategic flow of the deploying forces' equipment and sustainment from the aerial and sea port of embarkation and hand-off to the combatant commander in the aerial and sea port of debarkation (APOD and SPOD). The single port manager is responsible for providing strategic deployment status information to the combatant commander and to manage workload the APOD and SPOD operator based on the commander's priorities and guidance. The single port manager is responsible through all phases of the theater aerial and sea port operations continuum, from an unimproved airfield and bare beach deployment to a commercial contract supported deployment. Also called **SPM**. (JP 1-02)

staging—Assembling, holding, and organizing arriving personnel, equipment, and sustaining materiel in preparation for onward movement. The organizing and preparation for movement of personnel, equipment, and materiel at designated areas to incrementally build forces capable of meeting the operational commander's requirements. (JP 1-02)

stateless persons—Civilians who either have been denationalized, whose country of origin cannot be determined, or who cannot establish their right to the nationality claimed.

supporting commander—A commander who provides augmentation forces or other support to a supported commander or who develops a supporting plan. Includes the designated combatant commands and Defense agencies as appropriate. (JP 1-02)

supporting plan—An operation plan prepared by a supporting commander or a subordinate commander to satisfy the requests or requirements of the supported commander's plan. (JP 1-02)

sustainment—The provision of personnel, logistic, and other support required to maintain and prolong operations or combat until successful accomplishment or revision of the mission or of the national objective. (JP 1-02)

tactical level of war—The level of war at which battles and engagements are planned and executed to accomplish military objectives assigned to tactical units or task forces. Activities at this level focus on the ordered arrangement and maneuver of combat elements in relation to each other and to the enemy to achieve combat objectives. (JP 1-02)

theater—The geographical area outside the continental United States for which a commander of a combatant command has been assigned responsibility. (JP 1-02)

theater of operations—A subarea within a theater of war defined by the geographic combatant commander required to conduct or support specific combat operations. Different theaters of operations within the same theater of war will normally be geographically separate and focused on different enemy forces. Theaters of operations are usually of significant size, allowing for operations over extended periods of time. (JP 1-02)

theater of war—Defined by the National Command Authorities or the geographic combatant commander, the area of air, land, and water that is, or may become, directly involved in the conduct of the war. A theater of war does not normally encompass the geographic combatant commander's entire area of responsibility and may contain more than one theater of operations. (JP 1-02)

time-phased force and deployment data—The Joint Operation Planning and Execution System data base portion of an operation plan; it contains time-phased force data, non-unit-related cargo and personnel data, and movement data for the operation plan, including: **a.** In-place units. **b.** Units to be deployed to support the operation plan with a priority indicating the desired sequence for their arrival at the port of debarkation. **c.** Routing of forces to be deployed. **d.** Movement data associated with deploying forces. **e.** Estimates of non-unit-related cargo and personnel movements to be conducted concurrently with the deployment of forces. **f.** Estimate of transportation requirements that must be fulfilled by common-user lift resources as well as those requirements that can be fulfilled by assigned or attached transportation resources. Also called **TPFDD**. (JP 1-02)

APPENDIX C. REFERENCES AND RELATED PUBLICATIONS

North Atlantic Treaty Organization (NATO)

NATO Logistics Handbook

Joint Publications (JPs)

0-2	Unified Action Armed Forces (UNAAF)
1-02	Department of Defense Dictionary of Military and Associated Terms
1-06	Joint Tactics Techniques and Procedures for Financial Management During Jt Ops
2-0	Doctrine for Intelligence Support to Joint Operations
3-0	Doctrine for Joint Operations
3-07	Joint Doctrine for Military Operations Other Than War
3-07.3	JTTP for Peacekeeping Operations
3-08	Interagency Coordination during Joint Operations Vol II
3-10	Joint Doctrine for Rear Area Operations
3-10.1	Joint Tactics Techniques and Procedures for Base Defense
3-11	Joint Doctrine for Operations in Nuclear, Biological, and Chemical (NBC) Environments
3-16	Joint Doctrine for Multinational Operations
3-17	Joint Tactics, Techniques, and Procedures for Theater Airlift Operations
3-34	Engineer Doctrine for Joint Operations
3-35	Joint Deployment and Redeployment Operations
3-57	Doctrine for Joint Civil Affairs
4-0	Doctrine for Logistic Support of Joint Operations
4-01	Joint Doctrine for the Defense Transportation System
4-01.1	JTTP for Airlift Support to Joint Operations
4-01.2	JTTP for Sealift Support to Joint Operations
4-01.3	JTTP for Movement Control
4-01.4	Joint Tactics, Techniques, and Procedures for Joint Theater Distribution
4-01.5	Joint Tactics, Techniques and Procedures for Water Terminal Operations
4-01.6	Joint Tactics, Techniques, and Procedures for Joint Logistics Over-the-Shore (JLOTS)
4-01.7	Joint Tactics, Techniques, and Procedures for Use of Intermodal Containers in Joint Operations
4-01.8	Joint Tactics, Techniques, and Procedures for Joint Reception, Staging, Onward Movement, and Integration
4-02	Doctrine for Health Services in Joint Operations
4-02.1	JTTP for Health Services Logistic Support in Joint Operations
4-02.2	Joint Tactics, Techniques and Procedures for Patient Movement in Joint Operations

4-03	Joint Bulk Petroleum Doctrine
4-04	Joint Doctrine for Civil Engineering Support
4-05	Joint Doctrine for Mobilization Planning
4-06	Joint Tactics, Techniques, and Procedures for Mortuary Affairs in Joint Operations
4-07	Joint Tactics, Techniques, and Procedures for Common-User Logistics Support During Joint Operations
5-0	Doctrine for Planning Joint Operations
6-0	Doctrine for Command, Control, Communications, and Computer (C4) Systems Support to Joint Operations

Joint Military Operations Historical Collections

Chairman of the Joint Chiefs of Staff Manual (CJCSM)

3122.03	Joint Operation Planning and Execution System, Volume II, Planning Formats and Guidance

Joint Document

Joint Vision 2020

Marine Corps Doctrinal Publications (MCDPs)

1-0.1	Componency
1-2	Campaigning
3	Expeditionary Operations
4	Logistics
5	Planning
6	Command and Control

Marine Corps Warfighting Publications (MCWPs)

2-1	Intelligence Operations
3-32	Maritime Prepositioning Force (MPF) Operations
3-33.6	Procedures for Humanitarian Assistance Operations in Joint and Multi-Service Environments
3-40.3	Communications and Information Systems
3-41.1	MAGTF Rear Area Operations
4-1	Logistics Operations
4-11	Tactical-Level Logistics
4-11.1	Health Services Support Operations
4-11.4	Maintenance Operations
4-11.7	MAGTF Supply Operations
4-11.8	Services in an Expeditionary Environment
5-1	Marine Corps Planning Process

Marine Corps Reference Publications (MCRPs)

5-12A   Operational Terms and Graphics
5-12C   Marine Corps Supplement to Department of Defense
                     Dictionary of Military and Associated Terms

Marine Corps Intelligence Activity (MCIA) Publication

Generic Intelligence Requirements Handbook (GIRH)

Fleet Marine Force Manuals (FMFMs)

1-5/NWP 22-10   Maritime Prepositinging Force (MPF) Operations
4-6   Movement of Units in Air Force Aircraft

Marine Corps Orders (MCOs)

P3000.18   Marine Corps Planner's Manual
P4400.39G   War Reserve Materiel (WRM) Policy Manual
4900.3   Marine Corps Security Assistance

Marine Corps Miscellaneous Publications

U.S. Marines in Humanitarian Operations: Angels From the Sea:
    Relief Operations in Bangladesh
Humanitarian Operations: With the Marines in Operation Provide Comfort
Operational Maneuver From the Sea

Army Field Manuals (FMs)

3-100   Chemicals Operations Principles and Fundamentals
10-27   General Supply in Theaters of Operations
10-52   Water Supply in Theaters of Operations
10-67   Petroleum Supply in Theaters of Operations
54-23   Material Management
54-40   Area Support Group
55-9   Unit Air Movement Planning
55-10   Movement Control
63-3   Corps Support Command
63-11   Logistics Support Element Tactics, Techniques, and Procedures
90-31   AMCI Army and Marine Corps Integration in Joint Operations
100-9   Reconstitution
100-16   Army Operational Support
100-19   Domestic Support Operations
100-23-1   HA Multiservice Procedures for Humanitarian Assistance Operations

Miscellaneous

Goldwater-Nichols Department of Defense Reorganization Act of 1986
Conventional Forces in Europe Treaty